READER BONUS!

Dear Reader,

As a thank you for your support, Action Takers Publishing would like to offer you a special reader bonus: a free download of our course, "How to Write, Publish, Market & Monetize Your Book the Fast, Fun & Easy Way." This comprehensive course is designed to provide you with the tools and knowledge you need to bring your book to life and turn it into a successful venture.

The course typically **retails for $499**, but as a valued reader, you can access it for free. To claim your free download, simply follow this link ActionTakersPublishing.com/workshops - use the discount code "coursefree" to get a 100% discount and start writing your book today.

If we are still giving away this course by the time you're reading this book, head straight over to your computer and start the course now. It's absolutely free.

READER BONUS!

ActionTakersPublishing.com/workshops
discount code "coursefree"

EMBRACING THE IMPACT OF CANCER

Inspirational Stories of Hope

Copyright © Action Takers Publishing Inc 2023

All rights reserved. No part of this publication may be reproduced or transmitted in any form or by any means, mechanical or electronic, including photocopying and recording, or by any information storage and retrieval system, without permission in writing from publisher (except by reviewer, who may quote brief sections and/or show brief video clips in a review).

Disclaimer: The Publisher makes no representations or warranties with respect to the accuracy or completeness of the contents of this work and specifically disclaims all warranties, including without limitation warranties of fitness for a particular purpose. No warranty may be created or suitable for every situation. This works is sold with the understanding that the Publisher is not engaged in rendering legal, accounting, or other professional services. If professional assistance is required, the services of a competent professional person should be sought.

Neither the Publisher nor the Authors shall be liable for damages arising herefrom. The fact that an organization or website is referred to in this work as a referred source of further information does not mean that the Author or the Publisher endorse the information the organization or website may provide or recommendations it may make. Further, readers should be aware that websites listed in this work may have changed or disappeared between when this work was written and when it was read.

Email: lynda@actiontakerspublishing.com

Website: www.actiontakerspublishing.com

ISBN # (paperback) 978-1-956665-28-4
ISBN # (Kindle) 978-1-956665-29-1
Published by Action Takers Publishing™

DEDICATIONS

This book is dedicated to my friend Lanny Barker (1965-2018). When I was diagnosed with leukemia, he was going through chemo in the room next door and came over to let me know that I was not alone in my struggles and that there was hope. His example is one of the reasons I was inspired to offer a book such as this. We need each other to heal.

~Heather Carter

I dedicate this chapter in memory of Brodie Derrick, Nell Rinehart, and Beverly Smith whose battle ended way too early. And in honor of Todd F. Waites, my amazing husband and caregiver; Darden & Linda Sharp, my parents and caregivers, and Linda Waites, my mother-in-love and caregiver, thanks for all you did to support me along my cancer journey.

~Laura Sharp-Waites

DEDICATIONS

I dedicate this telling of my story to my Family and our collective Tribe. To Tom, you are my caregiver and co-adventurer. To Sydney, Catriona, Nataliya and Artur, you are my loves and my heartbeat. To our Tribe, you are my blessing and joy as this story continues to unfold.

~**Beca McPherson**

I would like to dedicate this chapter to all the people who rallied around me and continue to rally around me during this very difficult time. Your cards, care packages, meals, prayers and support have been invaluable. A special appreciation to my mom, Barbara, my children, Madison and Graham, and, most of all, to my husband Dan. You are all gifts from the God who holds us in His hands.

~**Debbie Burke**

To my loving husband and two daughters: you have always been by my side, cheering me on not only through my breast cancer journey but through life as we know it. You have taught me not to sweat the small stuff and it's ok to say, NO! To my sister, who drove a distance to be with me during my chemo treatments: words alone cannot express my gratitude. I Love You More!

~**Dina Legland**

I dedicate my chapter to all cancer survivors, notably my friend Lisa and my sweet grandma Patty, both of whom passed on during my treatment, I feel you. To all the caregivers, especially my own: Crystal, Jenn, mom (Marty), Mindy, and Chad, our teamwork made the journey possible, I see you. To the medical professionals who work in all areas surrounding cancer patient care, I am forever grateful, I thank you. And to those we will never stop fighting for, for more time with my loves Jaxon and Maya, Momma Jess will always be with you.

~**Jess Riney**

I dedicate my chapter to those that supported me through my journey. My family Aaron, Ebby, Xavier and Gabriel, Granny, my in-laws Rick and Sandy, and everyone that prayed for or helped us.

~**Lauren Engelke-Smith**

For my mother, Rebecca Knoles, a fellow survivor and the strongest woman I know. I am who I am because of you. Love you, Mom!

~**Lisa Woods**

To my husband Ron Carter. Always on my mind. Forever in my heart.

~**Pam Carter**

I dedicate my chapter to my big, beautiful, bay paint horse, Chance. A gift from my late husband, Chance has saved my life in more ways than one. It was while riding him one day that his back leg gave way slightly which resulted in me twisting and having back pain that oddly persisted. As it turned out, both Chance and I had serious, life-threatening health issues. The timing and duration of our illnesses were identical, but we are both rejuvenated in body and spirit and back in the saddle of life. With him I smile again and see that life truly is a gift and full of second Chances.

~Patti Schnoor

I dedicate this chapter to my wife, Jill, and to our four amazing children. They all walked with me step-by-step to beat cancer and without their support, I would not be here today. It was hard on us all, but we persevered and made it together!

~Ronn Hollis

In loving memory and with gratitude I dedicate this chapter to my hero grandfather, Ronald A. Mitchell, and my courageous mother, Kaaren L. Swindle. You touched so many during your lifetimes and my hope is, by sharing our story, your legacies continue throughout time. I miss and love you both.

~Tamara L. Hunter

TABLE OF CONTENTS

Introduction 1

Chapter 1: My Soul-Selfie by Heather Ann Carter 3

Chapter 2: We All Carry Shame, the Question Is How Much?
 by Laura Sharp-Waites 17

Chapter 3: Be Joyful in Hope by Debbie Burke 31

Chapter 4: Caretaker to Cancer Patient: Accepting Support
 on this Journey by Dina Legland 43

Chapter 5: Together We Can Do Anything by Jess Riney 55

Chapter 6: A Tragic Journey Full of Blessings
 by Lauren Engelke-Smith 67

Chapter 7: Check Your Boobs, Mine Tried to Kill Me
 by Lisa Woods 75

Chapter 8: Describe Your Journey of Being Impacted
 by Cancer by Pam Carter 85

Chapter 9: Embracing the Impact of Cancer by Patti Schnoor 97

Chapter 10: Choosing Unreasonable Hope
 by Rebecca S. McPherson 109

Chapter 11: Tools for the Fight by Ronn Hollis 123

Chapter 12: My Lung Cancer Story by Stephen Huff 131

Chapter 13: My Raison D'Etre After Cancer
 by Susan Sullivan Danenberger 141

Chapter 14: A Journey of Love by Tamara L. Hunter 151

INTRODUCTION

From Heather Ann Carter: I firmly believe that this compilation of inspiring stories from those who have gone to war with Cancer is invaluable. The primary purpose of this book is to encourage you or someone you know. Each author shares their unique perspective and source of strength that helped them triumph over the effects of this disease. Each of them has embraced the life-changing impact of it in some way. My prayer is that you will allow these messages to soothe your heart and share it with those who need to know that they're not alone in their struggles and that there's always hope.

From Laura Sharp-Waites: You have just heard a diagnosis that shakes your world, "You have cancer." I want you to know you are not alone on your journey. The authors in this book have been on similar cancer journeys and we know that what you are longing for most is hope, hope that everything will be okay. Hope can take on many different forms and meanings, but from my work with cancer patients as a pastoral counselor, I feel the one thing all cancer patients and their loved ones need is hope for today and tomorrow. Whether you're a cancer patient or walking with a loved one on a cancer journey, I pray that this book will offer the tools and encouragement you need.

CHAPTER 1

My Soul-Selfie

Heather Ann Carter

I remember it like it was last Thursday. I had been having symptoms for a few months. They had diagnosed me with rheumatoid arthritis. It still didn't seem right to us, but there was no other explanation for what I was experiencing.

It all came to a head after I returned from a trip to Napa to see my parents and siblings. I had gone on a hike with my sister and, during the hike, I felt like I was running a marathon. I don't remember all the symptoms I was experiencing while there, but I do remember our dear friend Claudia telling me I needed to get myself to the Mayo Clinic. There was clearly something else wrong.

When I got home, I had a hematoma the size of a salad plate on my leg. I had merely bumped it on a chair while in California. I also had bruises on my forearms from resting them on the armrests on the airplane.

Now, I'm no doctor, but that did not seem like rheumatoid arthritis to me!

Long story short, I went to the doctor the next week at eleven in the morning and by four they called and told me over the phone that my bloodwork was indicative of leukemia. They had a bed for me at the hospital and I needed to go there immediately. By five, I was sitting in a hospital room where I would remain for the next thirty-five days.

Because of the abruptness of this diagnosis, answering all the texts and calls soon got overwhelming, so my husband set up a blog to update people on the status of my cancer. This quickly morphed into me reflecting on the status of my soul. I did the writing myself until about week three, when I ended up intubated in the ICU for nine days with a secondary infection.

They weren't sure I was going to make it, so they flew my son, Berkeley, home from California where he had just started his freshman year of college at Biola.

My life, however, was spared because my husband, Blake, who is not a doctor, did some research (shout out to Web MD) and suggested they give me a neupogen shot that should boost my immune system. Once they gave that to me, I woke up a day or two later.

To this day, if Blake pushes back on anything I am doing, I find great pleasure in reminding him, "Hey, I don't want to hear any complaining. You had your chance, Buddy!"

I was still extremely sick when released from the ICU on March 3rd. When I woke up, I couldn't walk, talk, shower, roll over or eat by myself. I was forty-four years old and went home with a shower chair and a walker. In spite of that, the opening chapter in my first book is March 29.

Even though I wasn't sure if I would ultimately survive the Leukemia, I didn't want to wait to share with others what God was doing in me. I kept writing.

Through the reaction I got from those that read my blogs, I learned that I was not the only one who was struggling.

As I was preparing to write this chapter, I was reminded of a few lessons that a few years ago, I was forced to learn the hard way.

Much of what I am going to say comes from the books *Soul-Selfie* and *Soul-Selfie #NoFilter*. I published those books over the past few years. They are a collection of the blogs I started writing during my leukemia journey. The fact that I wrote anything that anyone would ever read and enjoy is a miracle in itself. I had never written anything before I had cancer and had never wanted to. But God gave me a gift, triggered by a terminal disease, in order to encourage others and come alongside them in their small and sometimes overwhelming life battles.

As it stands, even though my cancer is in remission, I am still soul-sick in many ways and will most likely never run out of material! At any given time, we are experiencing events in our lives involving trauma, drama, or the minutiae of everyday life. Learning how to integrate God into all of it is what I write about. It all counts. It's all a part of your story. It all matters and is useful in helping you connect with God and others.

I am passionate about walking alongside others as we learn how to let God have access to every nook and cranny of our lives.

For the purpose of this book, I want to focus on the first one – trusting in the TRAUMA: the most obvious and typical type of circumstances that trigger us to either abandon ourselves to God or too often, resent him.

Trauma is defined in Webster's Dictionary as a deeply distressing or disturbing experience. I think it's safe to assume we have all had our fair, or sometimes unfair, share of trauma.

I want to walk through some of the things I learned as a result of traveling that journey. There are just some things that can be learned in no other way but through suffering and reaching your proverbial bottom. Instant-pot lessons. The intense heat and pressures of life can transform us in ways that can take years to develop otherwise.

You may have been dealt the cancer card and are trying to find hope and strength for your journey like I was. Perhaps you are on the other side of it and are wondering what it was all for. How do you move forward and not waste what you went through? Unfortunately, cancer is not the only battle we will ever fight. I was hoping that was the biggie of my life, but as it turns out, life keeps dishing it out.

Because of this life-fact, it's imperative that we cling to this often hard-to-swallow truth: Regardless of what we go through, we always have a choice. We can get *BETTER* or we can get *BITTER*.

Here are some lessons I learned as I chose, one day at a time, to get *BETTER*.

1. Cultivate *community* before the *catastrophe*

I had gotten my real estate license right before my cancer diagnosis. Because of this, as prompted by my managing broker, I had written 100 handwritten notes, reconnecting with friends and members of our former church, many of whom I had not seen for years. I also got on social media for the first time.

By the time I was diagnosed with cancer two months later, I had laid the groundwork for the support that was imperative for my family during my cancer battle. Many of these people brought meals, prayed, picked up our kids, cleaned my house, and weeded my yard. (I'm still working on a scheme to get at least a couple of those perks back!)

One of the best illustrations of our need for community is a movie 127 Hours, with James Franco. It's about a guy who goes rock climbing and gets his hand wedged between the canyon wall and a giant boulder for, well, 127 hours.

At one point, he is videotaping himself. He basically talks about how sorry he was that he hadn't returned his mother's phone call the night before and how, in trying to appear like a super-hero and independent, he had told NO ONE where he was going. He concludes, "this rock has been waiting for me my whole life. I did this to *myself*."

(spoiler alert) When he finally saws off his own arm to set himself free, he comes across some other hikers. The camera zooms in on him yelling, "Heeeeeelp. (Gasp, choke, parched mouth.) I need HELP!"

We may feel like we can live life on our own, until disaster strikes, and we are lonely, exhausted and despairing. We need each other to navigate life; practically, emotionally, and spiritually. Don't wait until catastrophe strikes to build this foundation. Start now.

2. You can't *cram* for *serenity*

This is not a test that can be passed by pulling an all-nighter.

Any of you Seinfeld fans? In one episode, Kramer, Jerry Seinfeld's quirky neighbor, decides he can manage the stressful parts of his life by simply claiming, "serenity now."

George, one of their other friends, snarkily suggests that "serenity now equals *insanity* later."

So as trials and frustrations arise, Kramer calmly repeats the mantra "serenity now, serenity now." Until eventually, he just snaps and starts destroying everything around him in a rage screaming "serenity now!"

If we simply claim serenity, but don't ask God for it, it does indeed end in insanity. Though I believe God gives special graces and speaks gently and intimately to those in deep and dark places, **the longevity and health of your heart and soul depend on preparing now for what is to come.**

When disaster and death were at our doorstep, I knew exactly where my help and hope would come from.

As I spent seventy days admitted to the hospital over seven months, I was never really lonely because I knew my God and enjoyed his presence. I had been in a personal, consistent relationship with Him. I read spiritual literature regularly, prayed, attended bible studies and church services, and wrestled with him in the dark night of the soul. I had been training for this event for years.

I love how author Oswald Chambers puts it; *Crisis always reveals character.*

We have to put in the training time before the strain arises, if we are to be spiritually fit to endure it with faith and trust.

He says, in his 1915 vernacular:

"If you say 'I have no time for praying just now, no time for bible reading, my opportunity hasn't come yet'; when it does, of course I shall be all right. **No, you will not.** …"

To talk in this way is like trying to produce the munitions of war in the trenches, you will be killed while you are doing it. If we do not do the running steadily in the little ways, we shall do nothing in the crisis.

Start getting into fit spiritual shape now so you will be prepared for the inevitable marathons to come.

3. *Serve* **while** *sick*

This was the biggest *aha* that came to me as I struggled along my journey. I realized that even though I was battling the disease of cancer, my soul also had a disease and I wasn't the only one suffering from it. We all are actually soul sick. We all battle what I refer to as the common plagues of the heart. Plagues like worry, doubt, fear, control, resentment, just to name a few.

HOWEVER, we don't have to be 100% cured in order to help others. Today is not too soon to start serving others and sharing your story of strength and hope with those who need it.

I used to share in *hindsight*, but through this trauma I learned that others listen differently when I share out of my *messiness* rather than after I have gotten all cleaned up.

Several years ago, I remember listening to a podcast. The guy was talking about how he was asked to fill in as a biology professor at the last minute. He had zero schooling or training on the subject, but they were desperate, so he agreed. He would literally study the lesson the night before class, teach the topic the next day, and then go home and study for the following day's lesson. He learned brand new material every night and taught it the following day as if he had known the material for years.

One day, after class, an enamored young student came to him and said, "You are so amazing and smart and knowledgeable! I just wish I could know as much about biology as you do." The professor thought to himself, "Well, tomorrow, you will!"

I love that because I believe that's really all that's expected of us.

You may not be *cured*, but you might be one day ahead of someone else struggling with their disease,

a loveless marriage,

an addiction,

a tough boss or toxic co-worker,

an ailing parent or wayward child.

You don't need to have all the answers or even a solid belief that everything's going to be ok. You just need enough experience, strength and hope to help someone get through today. Over time, they can learn to carry this same message to others.

4. ***Uncertainty* is *certain***

Be acutely aware that you weren't in control of anything before the trauma came and knocked the wind out of you.

Before the cancer.

Or the divorce.

Or the addiction.

You were just delusional. And by delusional, I mean you were choosing to believe something that just wasn't true. That you had things under your control. You lived believing you were managing your little life pretty nicely.

The reality is, your situation was equally as precarious before things exploded. Or you imploded. You just weren't aware of it.

At any given time, our lives can be interrupted by events we didn't expect or plan for.

> *You, who say, 'today or tomorrow we will go to this or that city, spend a year there, carry on business and make money.' Why, you don't even know what will happen tomorrow ... what you ought to say is, 'if it is the Lord's will, we will live and do this or that.' As it is, you boast in your arrogant schemes.* James 4:13-15

You mistakenly think you are in complete control of your life.

So, what is the solution? Make your plans but hold them loosely. The fear that threatens to steal my sleep is arrested when I remember, and believe, that even though the future is uncertain, *God is not.*

My buddy, Oswald Chambers, laid it out for me in words that gave me clarity and comfort: "To be certain of God means that we are uncertain in all our ways, we do not know what a day may bring forth. This is generally said with a sigh of sadness, it should be rather an expression of breathless expectation. We are uncertain of the next step, but we ARE certain of God."

A friend of mine reminds me regularly that either *God is, or He isn't.* In other words, either you can trust him for everything or nothing at all. MY job is to draw close to God. To put myself under his care every day, in every situation, with everyone I love and everyone I have trouble loving.

I am hardly ever certain, even of what I am doing at that very moment. What I can know, and all I really have to know, is who God is and that

He is trustworthy. That does not mean I won't feel apprehensive about life once in a while. My human nature still tempts me to play God.

Around our house, there is a running joke aimed cruelly at me (and maybe a few of my friends) that I am *not always right, but I am always certain*. I may be completely off-base or flat-out wrong, but I will fight tooth and nail to get my way or have others acknowledge that I know what the heck I am talking about.

No comment.

What I really, really long to be is certain inside of uncertainty. Certain of God in the face of an uncertain future.

I will try to practice what Oswald suggests: "Leave the whole thing to God. It is gloriously uncertain how He will come in, but He will come. Remain loyal to Him."

5. *Pain* levels the *playing field*

When I was first admitted into the hospital, two different patients who had the same disease as me came into my room to tell me they knew how I felt and that they were there to support me.

I didn't know or care how old they were, if they had kids or who they voted for or even what religion they were. I just knew that we were suffering from the same sickness and that created an instant camaraderie that I had with no one else.

That's the reason the recovery community can rescue people who are threatened by addiction. They know that they are all suffering from the same disease that could literally kill them if they get sidetracked by anything other than their primary purpose of staying clean.

We need to stop posing and posturing and remember that we are all connected as fellow warriors, and let the rest fall away: Focus on our similarities, not the differences. There is so much that we can learn about ourselves and doing life with each other if we are willing to learn about, apply, and share the wisdom God has provided from *every* avenue of life He brings our way.

My life is richer and my perspective clearer as a result of what I have experienced in what some might call devastating circumstances. I truly wouldn't change a thing.

I want to button up things by reminding us that when trauma comes, it tries to trick us into believing we are the only one struggling. It whispers to us that we must have done something wrong or maybe God is disappointed in us.

I recently told one of my nurses that the last thing I remember saying before I ended up intubated in the ICU was, "I look like I'm going to have a baby," because my stomach was so distended from my infection.

She got teary and said, "Well, I remember the last thing you said to *me* was, 'what am I doing wrong?'"

It makes me very sad to think that I suspected I had done something bad to cause that kind of suffering. Many people out there believe that when they suffer, they must be doing something wrong, and that God is punishing them. That's when I try to remind myself, and others, that the "Rain falls on the just and the unjust." My paraphrase of that is "Good things happen to bad people and bad things happen to good people." What we do with those things and what we learn from them depends on how we partner with God in the redemption of it.

Our temptation is to pout, over-medicate, over-control, numb-out, or isolate. We get so hyper-focused on trying to navigate and fix the situation that we neglect our bodies and souls and even our relationship with the God we once thought we could trust.

This is a common reaction. It's *normal* to go there, but not safe to *stay* there. When hard times come, we have a choice. Like I said, we can get *better* or we can get *bitter*.

If you attempt to apply some of these lessons to your own trauma, maybe you can get to the hopeful part more quickly, without having to trudge slowly through the confusion and the despair.

As I say in my books, in a thousand different forms, we are all "In this together."

My prayer is that as you read the following stories you will join us in "Embracing the Impact of Cancer."

Heather Ann Carter

Heather Carter was born into a family of joy and faith, raised in the Pacific Northwest, finally settling in Napa, California, for junior high and high school. It was there she met future husband, Blake. They set off to college in Missouri and then finally graduated school in Illinois, settling in Springfield, Illinois, where Blake entered into full-time ministry in a local church and their family was born: two sons and a daughter.

Her primary career and passion, when her children were little, was her family, but she also had the opportunity to serve in a number of leadership roles within the church community as well as in the workplace both as a special needs assistant and executive admin.

As her kids began to enter the college years, she decided she would try her hand as a realtor. That's when her world turned upside down with her leukemia diagnosis in 2015. God got her through that and she is now a survivor. Through that experience, she's had an opportunity to produce a blog that has now run over seven years, has reached over 20,000 people and produced two books, *Soul-Selfie* and *Soul-Selfie: #NoFilter*. Her speaking and writing has taken her across the country and she loves nothing more than sitting down with people and sharing stories of hope.

Connect with Heather at www.heathercarterwrites.com.

CHAPTER 2

We All Carry Shame, the Question Is How Much?

Laura Sharp-Waites

Embrace: *To clasp, or hold close with the arms, usually as an expression of affection.*

I can envision embracing my spouse, a fur baby, a friend, or even a relative. But how do we embrace something that's trying to kill us? It's challenging for sure.

Even today, people with health challenges, such as cancer, struggle and keep their diagnosis a secret from friends, colleagues, and even family, not wanting to share their personal health information. I get that, but it's really more than that.

Cancer doesn't discriminate, and neither does shame. Many people, including me, have experienced self-blame around a cancer diagnosis, and some may even experience feelings of embarrassment or shame. Having cancer is difficult, but adding feelings of guilt, shame, or embarrassment on top of other painful emotions, like sadness and anxiety, only intensifies that difficulty. Unfortunately, these are all very natural feelings.

I think it's important for us to recognize that shame differs from guilt. Shame is a painful emotion caused by the belief that one is, or is perceived to be, inferior or unworthy of affection, love, or respect because of one's actions, thoughts, circumstances, or experiences. While shame focuses on the self or person, guilt focuses on behavior. Thinking of it like this, shame is *I'm a bad person because of this behavior*, versus guilt being *I feel badly about a behavior.*

Feelings of shame can especially come up with cancers that may be linked to specific behaviors, whether or not those behaviors actually played a role in the diagnosis. For example, people might ask a person with lung cancer, "Did you smoke?" This question is unhelpful, whether the person smoked or not.

During my breast cancer journey, I heard a number of shaming experiences from other cancer patients:

> A man shared with me that several people told him he could have avoided prostate cancer by eating healthy and exercising. That comment made him feel horrible and was not helpful or hopeful.
>
> My husband was asked if he was going to stay with me because I wasn't whole anymore! Not whole???
>
> Another example was a woman I meet during treatments with oral cancer. She felt ashamed about her diagnosis and the fact that the surgeries had left her face disfigured. She was in tears one morning and

> when I asked her if she was ok, she said her husband had her served with divorce papers earlier in the day.

Wow! Let's just kick the person while they are already down.

Humans are meaning-making beings, by this I mean as humans we want to understand how something happens so we can attempt to have some control over it and even stop it from reoccurring. But cancer can happen to anyone. It's an illness, not a failure on our behalf. These feelings can also come up in people who have cancer in a body part that isn't often discussed openly. For example, an individual with colorectal cancer may require help using the bathroom or cleaning up after appliance leaks, which may cause embarrassment. Or perhaps it is a woman with a gynecological cancer or breast cancer which may include sexual side effects that take a toll on her confidence and self-esteem.

Getting to the Root of Shame

Untangling shame starts with helping individuals identify where their negative thoughts are coming from. These negative thoughts could be related to messages they received from their parents or other caretakers when they were young or from society in general. For example, we learn at a young age that our genitals are private, and that bathroom behavior and sexual habits are not topics for discussion.

We get all kinds of messages about body parts that we aren't supposed to talk about, and the only language we really have to discuss is either pornographic or detail oversharing, or very clinical, using medical terminology. This is when our private details are made public, and that can be very uncomfortable. These are learned thoughts and it is important to understand how someone takes the information and processes it.

Individuals might also hold certain beliefs about how the world works or how much control they have over their own lives. They might think their cancer is a punishment or payback for something they did. During my cancer journey, I experienced several comments from faith-based individuals who asked me, "What did you do for God to give you cancer?" Of course, they were making referencing to Job. Sadly, these individuals did not have a good grasp of the Scripture they were referencing, or they would have known that God did not give Job his series of tragedies. God allowed Satan to bring on these tragedies as a test of Job's faith in God. My response was that God did not give me cancer, but He allowed me to have it and my experience was going to glorify Him.

The good news is that all of these harmful beliefs can be unlearned. Once people understand more about where their negative thoughts are coming from, they can begin challenging and removing them. These thoughts may not totally go away, but we experience them differently. Here is an analogy; automatic thoughts are a well-worn path in the brain, like a trail in the woods. It's easy to walk down the trail because it's so familiar. It doesn't mean there aren't any other trails to follow, but it just takes time to build them.

No cancers are alike and each of us have a different DNA which requires a unique treatment plan just for you. Telling the patient how your aunt or friend approached their cancer battle is not helpful. All of these comments, although most of the time are well intended, serve to make patients feel that if they had done everything right, they wouldn't have cancer. I spent significant time explaining to my friends that my cancer wasn't bad luck, that I didn't do anything to deserve it, and that most likely nothing could have been done to prevent it. However, after comments about exercise from friends, comments from well-meaning family and friends regarding surgery choices and chemotherapy, there was still plenty of blame directed at me.

You Are Not Alone

Shame thrives in isolation. When we think we are the only one dealing with something, we may heap even more negative feelings onto ourselves. In my Pastoral Counseling and Coaching work, I help women recognize that they are not alone in their experiences.

Shame has to do with your relationship with yourself and your relationships with others. Someone might think, "Are people going to judge me because of my cancer? Am I going to belong with what I have gone through?" These questions are normal because belonging is one of our deepest human needs.

When doing group work, I often ask, "How many of you have felt this way?" When others see hands go up, it helps the speaker feel less alone. Our society rewards those who are brave; therefore, we are not encouraged to let others in on our pain. Our culture tells us vulnerability is bad, but it takes a lot of strength to own your experience, which helps us reframe some of these thoughts.

Handling Cancer Your Way

Everyone's cancer experience is different. I have noticed four types of people on a cancer journey: 1) those who are very open about what they have been through; 2) those who take on the battle with a vengeance and become advocates after their healing; 3) those who bury their head in the sand like an ostrich, not wanting to know anything about what is going on with the cancer or treatment; and 4) some just want to move on with their lives. There is not one single way to walk this journey. I have met women who have been on all three of those paths during their cancer. People can find different ways of making meaning out of their experience. It is all about how much you want to incorporate this part of your story into your life. Your cancer story is one slice of the pie, but you get to decide how big a slice it is.

Today, we see women who feel blamed for having cancer. The society we live in has created a culture of blame shaming and it could not be worse when it comes to living with cancer. Shame is that terrible, private feeling that something is wrong with us, that we are somehow defective as a person. That we are broken, beyond repair, or damaged and that if anyone really knew what we were like, we would be rejected.

A part of the experience of shame is the fear of being found out and exposed. We want to run, hide, and protect ourselves from exposure to other people's judgement. I experienced moments of shame for having breast cancer. I had feelings of being somehow less than as a woman for experiencing breast cancer. Shame is the result of a lie you believe about yourself. Shame can influence your life in a bad way. It creates many false beliefs that can lead you to hide out from yourself and others. At the beginning of my cancer journey, I knew that I would be having reconstruction surgery so, thankfully, I never felt like I wouldn't be whole after the process. It was only after having my ovaries removed because of cancerous cysts, that I realized I would never be able to have biological children. In the Bible, children are a gift from God and are blessings, blessings I would never know.

When most people experience shame, they want to hide. It is normal to want to isolate yourself when you are feeling shame. Although the feeling is common, that doesn't mean it's the best choice. A better option would be to let out your shame. When you share your story with others, they can speak the truth of God's love over you. You can let it go and ask for the support you need.

When you're living with shame, it can be easy to let it dominate your thoughts. You may find yourself thinking unkind thoughts about yourself when things go wrong. You might say something like, "Of course this happened, I'm meant to suffer." Or "I deserve to suffer!" Changing your thoughts isn't easy, as it usually takes a while before you feel like you are making any progress. Think of it as learning a new language, the language of God's compassion.

Shame Can Affect Our Decisions for Years

When I remembered the women, I know who are breast cancer survivors, I could see that I was being entirely irrational. You see these women were some of the most beautiful humans I know. The most important thing for me was not to figure out where these feelings of shame were coming from but to just let them go!

In a shame culture, you know you are good or bad by what your community says about you. By contrast, in a guilt culture, you know you are good or bad by how you feel about your behavior and choices. Female patients with breast cancer feel they are shamed by others and feel blamed for their cancer because of the current ads and articles that focus heavily on prevention being the key. These ads and articles focus on women and attempt to show everything one can do to prevent cancer with a not-so-subtle suggestion in the word prevention. Basically, if the woman had done everything right, she could have prevented her breast cancer.

These ads and articles try to educate on the more appropriate terms of risk reduction for an individual's ability to decrease the chance of breast cancer, but this risk is never zero. It is not even zero in the most extreme cases, for example, when someone may have a bilateral mastectomy. Regardless internet, news stories, magazine article, daytime talk shows, and health food advertisements all advise women of things they could do to prevent breast cancer. Satan wants to convince you that you are alone in your shame. He wants you to feel as if you are the only one to ever experience it and he wants that feeling of shame to keep you isolated so you don't turn to your loving Savior. Thankfully, you are not alone in shame. As part of his death on the Cross, Jesus experienced every human emotion, including shame and humiliation.

Women and Shame

As women, we are prone to shame. We feel we have to look a certain way, act a certain way, and smell a certain way. From an early age, we are taught to be people pleasers, to not rock the boat, to not be assertive, to care a lot about what others think, and to mold ourselves into what we are told by others and society to be. We can feel shame for working, for not working, for having children, for not having children, for letting our hair go gray, for coloring our hair, for making meals from scratch, for using pre-packaged foods in meals, for not working overtime enough at work, for not smelling fresh out of a shower, for wearing the right lipstick, or for having the right eyebrows. And to add to my shame, my eyebrows didn't fall out during chemo, they waited until six months after and then fell out. Sadly, years later and my eyebrows have not fully grown back.

We care about what others think and try to mold ourselves into other's images. How many mothers think they are not good mothers and carry mother guilt? How many women feel shame for not being able to do it all? For being too big or weighing too much? Yes, we as women are prone to shame and shame can be used by others, both consciously and unconsciously, to motivate us.

How many of us shame ourselves with our negative self-talk or make decisions based on avoiding feeling shame? From ourselves and others? How many of us are still trying to prove our mothers, fathers, coaches, society, bosses, or someone else wrong? We as women can be held hostage by shame. The lies of shame want us to believe that we are defective, not enough, that something is wrong with us. God wants us to believe that we are his treasure, loved beyond measure. Truth crushes the lies of shame.

Effects Of Shame

Shame causes our self-esteem to shrink to nothing. We see ourselves as seriously flawed. Unworthy. Worthless. Shame makes us doubt ourselves, our abilities, and even the core of who we are. It causes us to hide. We don't want anyone to know our secrets, that if exposed, would cause others to run from us or withdraw their love. The sneaky thing about shame is that it can haunt us for years, resurfacing, and reminding us of our inadequacy years after the event.

Individuals are continually judged by the decisions they make in response to their cancer diagnosis. I cannot tell you how many times I have been told I should not feel bad about not being able to have biological children because there are so many children in foster care who need to be adopted. Sadly, this statement only hurts more because they are trying to negate my grief by not acknowledging it.

I certainly did not choose to have cancer, but I did choose to undergo the medical procedures to combat it. Most women with breast cancer don't even have the option of choosing to not have surgery, but they are still judged on whether they selected lumpectomy or mastectomy. Despite studies clearly showing that breast conservation and radiation have outcomes just as successful than mastectomy in terms of recurrence, patients are chastised by friends and family with, "You need to be aggressive" or "You'll never forgive yourself if it comes back" when they have selected breast conservation. I had a lumpectomy and was not able to get clear margins, so I had a mastectomy. Either way, someone I knew was going to be upset with my decision.

Judgment doesn't stop even when patients choose aggressive courses of treatment. People who want bilateral mastectomies for symmetric reconstruction or select mastectomy over lumpectomy to avoid radiation are judged for overreacting and doing more than was necessary. In many cases, patients with cancer get blamed no matter what they do, and the goal posts are always shifting.

There is another group of patients with breast cancer who face significant prejudice with their diagnosis: men. Some of the decisions I have mentioned such as surgical choice, etc., are issues that women often struggle with more, but men face the same judgments about treatment choices, lifestyles, and work pressures with the added burden of having what many consider a woman's cancer.

As I mentioned earlier, most breast cancer ads are targeted to women, but there is a different kind of pain and judgment when one is excluded all together and dismissed for even being at risk for this type of cancer. People ask male patients, "How did you even get a woman's cancer?" or ask them to show up to an area of the hospital for imaging that warns **women only**, and then add insult to injury by giving them the only type of gown available, yep you guessed it- a pink one.

One very simple change we could make is to choose our words precisely: we can speak of *risk reduction* instead of *prevention*, and clarify that *treatments fail patients* and *patients do not fail treatments*.

If you want to live free, you'll need to unpack your shame, examine it, and discover its source. As you realize where your shame is coming from, you can continue to seek God's healing. God longs to release you from shame and other negative emotions so you can experience His deep love and abiding peace. Romans 5:5 says, *And hope does not put us to shame, because God's love has been poured out into our hearts through the Holy Spirit, who has been given to us.*

Laura Sharp-Waites

Laura Sharp-Waites, M. Ed., MDiv., Ed. D, is a Pastoral Counselor, Transformational Grief Coach, Author, and Speaker. Helping people has always been a gift for Laura. For many years, she was a Special Education Teacher, College Professor, and Pastor supporting people of all ages and walks of life through a myriad of personal, professional, and spiritual struggles. Now, Laura focuses on helping Christian women heal from sorrow, trauma, or abuse.

In her 90-Day Program, Pieces to Peace: Dare To Live Again, Laura shares how to:

- overcome feelings of shame, guilt, unworthy, and worthless
- live without numbing agents
- avoid self-harm
- navigate their new normal
- move forward

- learn how to trust again

- feel peace, comfort, and security

- and handle the hard days, and the days in between

Laura has authored two journal articles and two books including one International Best-Selling book.

Laura now blends her extensive educational experience and certifications to help her clients. Laura holds a number of certifications, a Master's in Special Education, a Master's in Divinity: Pastoral Counseling, and a Doctorate in Organizational Leadership.

Laura enjoys spending time with her husband Todd, her parents, mother-in-law, and critters – Roscoe and Sassy. When not working, you can find her reading several books, doing a Bible Study, cooking, baking, spending time in the North Carolina/Tennessee Mountains, and enjoying a good cup of coffee!

Connect with Laura at www.LauraSW.com.

CHAPTER 3

Be Joyful in Hope

Debbie Burke

Many of the stories you read in this book are from the perspective of someone who has gone through cancer and is now cancer free. They are on the other side of the storm. The dark and scary clouds have parted, and they can look back, see things clearly, and can tell you how they pulled through. I, however, write from the middle of the storm. Ten months ago, I was diagnosed with stage 4b ovarian cancer. It is the worst diagnosis you can receive for this type of cancer. Here is my story…

In January of 2022, I noticed blood in my stool. It didn't concern me at first. This had happened before, and it always went away. Except it didn't. In February 2022, I called my primary care doctor and got a phone consultation. He wasn't worried either. Fourteen months earlier I'd had a perfect colonoscopy. By the end of February, however, I started to worry and called the gastrointestinal practice directly. A doctor could not see me for two months, but I could see a PA the next week. I made the appointment with the PA who immediately ordered a repeat colonoscopy.

Scheduled for March 17th, St. Patrick's Day, I laughed my head off when I learned the physician to perform the procedure was named *Dr. Patrick O'Reilly!* What a way to celebrate the Irish! While prepping for the colonoscopy, I thought about what a good practical joke it would be to add green dye to all the liquids I had to drink and give Dr. O'Reilly a real St. Patrick's Day joy ride! While I love a good joke, I didn't want to impact his ability to see in my colon.

When I woke up from the procedure, Dr. O'Reilly came into the recovery room and told me the worst, most shocking news: he had seen cancer in my colon, a three-centimeter tumor. The samples went to the lab for biopsy. The luck of the Irish was NOT with me that St. Patrick's Day!

Early the next morning, we got bloodwork taken and then headed to the airport to pick up my mom, sister, and her husband who were flying in to see my niece play volleyball, a visit of which had been planned for weeks. My brother was already in town with his wife and daughter. They all live more than eight hours away by car, and it was the first time they were all in my city in almost twelve years. On the way to the airport, Dr. O'Reilly called with some strange news. The biopsy showed that this was not colon cancer. It was some other type of cancer, what type was not immediately known. The cells were odd. Perhaps the scan planned for later that day would show us more.

We got my family settled at home. What was supposed to be a super-fun weekend now had an ominous feel. My husband and I headed to another medical center for the CT scan. In less than thirty minutes we were done, and on the way home, Dr. Reilly called again. The pathologist thought it was some type of female cancer, but wasn't completely sure. It being a Friday, he would get back to me on Monday. However, within an hour of being scanned, the CT results hit my patient portal. The radiologist had already read my scan and loaded the results where I could access them. I logged into my portal, and without help or explanation from any doctor, began to read the findings.

The report was long, and the cancer was everywhere. There were four different five-centimeter tumors on both ovaries, in the uterus, and around the pelvic area. One of these tumors had grown and invaded the colon, causing the bleeding that prompted my investigation. There were a couple of tumors in lymph nodes, a two-centimeter tumor in my liver, and another two- centimeter tumor in my spleen, plus small tumors all over the peritoneal tissue in my abdomen. My oncologist would later describe it like someone took a handful of pea gravel and threw it at my abdomen where it stuck, all over the place.

My husband and I were shocked. Reading this report alone, without the help of a physician, was quite unsettling. I knew I needed an oncologist, so, unsure of what to do, I texted a friend whose husband was a lung surgeon. I read to him the results of my CT scan. Unbeknownst to me, he was a partner in an oncology practice, so, he called one of his partners who fit me in for an appointment on Tuesday, four days later.

Having my whole family in town for the weekend was helpful. I received support from all the people who love me most, while also getting the worst medical news ever. We attended church together on Sunday and the sermon was entitled *Do Not Lose Heart* from 2 Corinthians 4:1-18. It was encouraging and included points like *Refuse to trust in your own strength* and *Refuse to give in to despair*. Listening to this was both faith-building and challenging, and it gave me hope.

Some of my family left on that Sunday, and I couldn't help but cry saying goodbye to my mom on the following Monday. My husband took me to the oncologist on Tuesday and her words were tough to hear:

"This is ovarian cancer."

"Stage 4b."

"Very aggressive."

"We hope we can manage it."

"There is no cure."

She explained how cancer can spread through blood or the lymph system. I had cancer in lymph nodes and in my spleen, so I knew this cancer was already spreading on both superhighways. The first bit of work was to go to The Mayo Clinic for surgery.

The Sunday before heading to Mayo, I went to church again. This week the title of the sermon was *Facing Death with Confidence* from 2 Corinthians 5:1-10.

Really?!?!?

I gasped out loud.

"God, what are you telling me? This sermon blows up last week's sermon called Do Not Lose Heart *because now I am losing heart!"* I did not know if I could stay in the service, but I did, and although hard to hear, the message was true. We learned that:

1. There are limitations on our earthly bodies. We are all subject to destruction one day. No one lives forever.

2. While we are in our earthly bodies, we operate in faith. Upon death, followers of Christ will join Him in heaven. This is a guarantee. We can have good courage despite the trials we face.

3. Someday we will all appear before the judgment seat of Christ. If one is a believer, Jesus has borne the judgment for our sins.

While I believe all this to be true and comforting, I was only fifty-five when I learned I had stage 4 ovarian cancer. My kids are in their early twenties. I want to see them get married. I want to know my grandchildren. I asked God for mercy and to give me more time.

Following church, the elders and several friends gathered to pray for me. This is a practice based on James 4:14-15 which says, *Is anyone among you sick? Let them call the elders of the church to pray over them and anoint them with oil in the name of the Lord. And the prayer offered in faith will make the sick person well; the Lord will raise them up. If they have sinned, they will be forgiven.*

It was a sweet time of prayer. Many people prayed and I felt very supported.

The next morning, I was at Mayo sitting with the surgeon. Initially she told me that my cancer was very advanced, and they did not think they could operate. They thought instead they should send me back to the oncologist for chemo. After further evaluation, however, they believed operating first would give me the best chance. The next day, I had a nine and a half hour surgery. They believed they had gotten ninety-eight to ninety-nine percent of the cancer, but they could not get it all. They removed my ovaries, fallopian tubes, uterus, and my spleen; they removed and re-sectioned part of my colon; they shaved off part of my liver and removed a couple of lymph nodes, as well as all the tissue lining my abdomen and my appendix. As one nurse said, "There isn't much left in there."

Post-op recovery was long and painful. My incision started at my sternum and ended at my pubic bone. Everything hurt. Every movement hurt. Despite the pain, the nurses had me up and walking that very night! Even in this moment of physical devastation, I did have a sweet peace that God was with me, and I was encouraged by many notes sent through CaringBridge and cards. Five days later, I was discharged to finish my recovery at home.

Less than one month after surgery and before I was completely recovered, I started chemo. It was only once every three weeks, but it lasted all day long. A good friend of mine who lived twelve hours away was diagnosed with breast cancer a couple of weeks after I was diagnosed with ovarian cancer. We frequently ended up in the chemo chair at the same time. We texted each other updates, shared symptoms, and Bible verses to encourage each other along the way. It was helpful having someone to talk to who understood what I was going through, because she was going through it too.

After four and a half months of chemo, a scan could not detect cancer in my body. Three months after that scan, another one did slightly - light up - in one spot. Eight weeks later a third scan said I was still all clear. This was a HUGE relief. I am officially N.E.D., which means -no evidence of disease. For a stage 4 diagnosis, this is extremely good. But with stage 4 cancer, they will never call you cured. I will scan again in three months. If something appears to be growing, the oncologist will want to put me back into chemo. Hopefully, I will be clear again and stay off chemo. Scans like this will continue for the rest of my life.

The title of this book is *Embracing the Impact of Cancer*. When initially asked to be a contributor, I did not know if I could honestly say that I'd embraced anything about cancer. But as one who is ten months into a scary storm with clouds and high waves, this is what I would recommend to embrace to someone who is newly diagnosed:

1. **Embrace acceptance**. When first diagnosed with cancer, shock and denial hit powerfully, but you must push through them fast and

accept the fact that you are dealing with a life-threatening disease. Without this sober realization, you can't look toward what you need to do to heal. When I got home after surgery, I was perusing in my bookcase and saw the book *Cancer: Biblical Truths that Bring Comfort*. I had purchased it to have it on hand in case a friend was diagnosed with cancer, and of course I had no idea the book would be for me. Each chapter is based on a word. The first chapter's word is *Acceptance*, and it says this, "Acceptance is the last stage of grief. It is the most difficult of the stages for people to reach. Accepting something does not signify one's giving up, but it does address that there is a problem, and you're ready to deal with it. Cancer is one of the biggest problems you may ever face, but know that you are loved by a God that accepts you and loves you and will walk with you through this time. When we accept this, then we can start moving forward with Him." When I first read this, I was very angry. Accept cancer? Are you kidding me? I did not want to accept cancer, I wanted to reject cancer! But rejecting cancer is simply hanging out in a state of denial, which makes you unable to cope and move forward. So, embrace acceptance and face your cancer head on.

2. **Embrace Grief**. Just because you've accepted the fact that you have cancer doesn't mean you are done grieving. Cancer causes you to lose a lot, and grieving is the normal response to loss. When my oncologist told me I would come to know a *new normal*, I cried. I did not want a new normal! I wanted the normal I'd always had. So, when circumstances change and are hard, I allow myself to grieve.

    - When I first saw my huge scar down the middle of my body, I grieved. Not that I wore bikinis a lot, but this permanently changed me, and I needed to cry about it.

- When my hair fell out and I became bald, I grieved. I'd always had long brown hair. I really liked my hair. Watching it come out by the fistful in the shower was traumatic. Now I didn't have any hair and the wig just wasn't the same. When you look in the mirror and don't recognize the person looking back at you, it's OK to grieve.

- When the side effects of chemo hit me hard and I had to stay home for days at a time, I grieved. Missing out on the things that I normally did was difficult. I let myself grieve these losses.

Cancer takes and takes and takes. When you feel these losses deeply, embrace grief!

3. **Embrace Uncertainly.** After a couple of cycles of chemo, I sort of lost it. The side effects were hard, and I was in a lot of pain. My feelings were intense and ran the gamut:

"I am in a lot of pain!"

"Is it good pain or bad pain?"

"Is the chemo working?"

"Is the cancer dying?"

'Is the cancer spreading?"

"Will I make it through treatment?"

"My mom is renting a house in Florida for Thanksgiving; will I even be there?"

"I **HATE** living in all of this uncertainty!!!!"

My husband just looked at me and said, "Things have always been uncertain, Debbie, you have just been living under the illusion that some things are certain. Now that you have cancer, you can't do that anymore."

He was right!

When I didn't have cancer, I wasn't faced with the reality that life can be taken from me at any moment. With cancer, that fact seems very real. But when you embrace uncertainty, you learn to enjoy the present and appreciate all the moments you are experiencing without fearing what could be ahead. After all, no one knows what will happen tomorrow. Even people without cancer.

Years ago, I worked with a woman whose dad had cancer. He went through all the chemo treatments and was determined to be cancer-free. He rang the bell at the chemo lab, and everyone celebrated that he was cured! Twelve weeks later, he was hit by a drunk driver and killed in a car accident. Beating cancer didn't give him any certainty about his future.

So, embrace uncertainty! Eat, drink, and be merry. Enjoy the present day and each special moment. No one knows what tomorrow holds!

4. **Embrace all your treatment options**. People have strong opinions on this. On one extreme, you have the people only willing to pursue conventional treatment and think the alternative folks are all quacks. On the other extreme, you have alternative/natural people who think the conventional doctors are modern-day sorcerers putting poison in your veins. Neither extreme is 100 percent right or helpful.

While I've gone conventional, I'm doing some alternative things, too. This includes working with someone who can help me with my diet to make sure I'm getting the best nutrition for my body while it is withstanding very strong treatments. Your oncologist will likely tell you to eat whatever you want. This is bad advice. They have almost zero training in nutrition.

I also read about the dangers of amalgam fillings in alternative literature. I had eight amalgam fillings in my mouth that were forty to fifty years old. They release mercury, a toxic heavy metal, into your system. Alternative practitioners are adamant that these need to come out or you won't recover from cancer. So, I had all my amalgam fillings removed and replaced with composite, non-toxic fillings. I don't know if this will help me heal, but all these old fillings had decay underneath. They needed to be replaced even if I didn't have cancer. Not one conventional doctor recommended this course of action. I learned it all through alternative sources.

Do not limit your treatment options to one extreme or another. Explore everything available and <u>embrace</u> what treatment options are best for your situation.

5. **Embrace Hope.** Depending on whose statistics you believe, I have a seventeen to thirty-one percent chance of living five years. Those are not good odds. But doctors are frequently wrong, and I've met and read about a lot of people who have beat the odds. I've even met a woman who had stage 4 ovarian cancer and was given a five percent chance of living five years… that was in 1991! And she's alive and healthy in 2023! She had hope and to beat the odds, hope is important. There are a lot of studies that confirm that cancer patients with no hope do not fare well.

I don't know how long I'll live. I hope I will also have one of those amazing *against-all-odds* stories. At the same time, I have faced the reality that no one gets through life without death. Ultimately, my hope is in my faith in Jesus Christ, who will carry me home to heaven when my earthly body gives out.

So, my wish for you, dear Reader, is that you will <u>embrace hope</u> as you face your cancer challenge. I will pray these two prayers for you, and recommend you pray them for yourself:

Be joyful in <u>hope</u>, patient in affliction, faithful in prayer.
(Romans 12:12, NIV)

May the God of <u>hope</u> fill you with all joy and peace in believing, so that by the power of the Holy Spirit you may abound in <u>hope</u>.
(Romans 15:13, ESV)

Debbie Burke

Debbie Burke is a wife to Dan for thirty-four years and a mom to Madison and Graham, two young adults in their mid-twenties. She holds a BS in Business Education from the University of Illinois and an MA in Communication from the University of Missouri. While she worked almost ten years in private & public sector training and education, for most of her career Debbie has been a stay-at-home mom and corporate housewife, living in eight locations, including a four-year stint in Warsaw, Poland. More recently, you could find her teaching women's Bible studies at her church in Eden Prairie, Minnesota.

Follow Debbie and her cancer journey on CaringBridge at https://www.caringbridge.org/visit/debbieburke2.

CHAPTER 4

Caretaker to Cancer Patient: Accepting Support on this Journey

Dina Legland

The Phone Call

One night in September 2016, I was standing at the kitchen sink washing dishes after dinner, and all of a sudden I got a sharp, stabbing pain in my right breast. I yelled in pain and grabbed my chest. My husband asked, "What's the matter? Are you having a heart attack?" I said, "No, I feel like somebody's stabbing me with a knife." When the pain finally subsided, I felt my right breast, and found an odd-shaped lump. Having coped with cystic, dense breasts with calcifications for a long time, I thought maybe it was just another cyst. This felt different from anything I've ever felt before. It was actually in the shape of the letter "C," and from what I could tell at the time, it was about an inch long. My husband said to me, "Tomorrow, call the doctor and set up an appointment." I said I would. What I didn't tell him was that for the last two weeks, I was getting these sharp, stabbing pains intermittently, and that they weren't happening six months prior when I had my last mammogram.

By the next day, I wanted to just put it out of my mind. I kept telling myself that it's probably just another cyst, and I shouldn't worry about it. I'm scheduled for another mammogram in February. Once I got to work, I saw a dear friend and colleague. I happened to mention it to her, and I figured it couldn't hurt to ask for her opinion. I trusted her immensely, as years before she had been diagnosed with breast cancer and treated with radiation and a lumpectomy. She actually examined the lump, and as soon as she did she said, "Let's call the doctor." I called right away, and I was scheduled for the next day.

On Wednesday, I saw the doctor who conducted a physical exam, and then scheduled a sonogram for Thursday. Once the sonogram was done, the doctor wouldn't let me leave. She ordered an immediate 3D mammogram. After waiting two to three hours for the results, the radiologist said, "You need a needle biopsy and I'm scheduling it for tomorrow." I had the biopsy on Friday. These results were going to take a little bit longer, so I had to get through the weekend with no answers. I didn't know how long the results would take. The only people who knew about this were my husband, two daughters and my colleague.

By Monday with still no news, I went to work. On my way home, the phone rang. When I answered, I heard a voice say, "Dina, where are you?" I said, "I'm driving home from work." The voice told me to "pull over to the side of the road." At that point, I knew it wasn't going to be good news. On Monday, October 10, 2016, the radiologist said to me, "I'm sorry to be the one to tell you this, but you have an aggressive form of breast cancer. You need to see a breast surgeon and oncologist immediately." Needless to say, the hour-long drive home was torture. All I could think about was how am I going to tell my husband and daughters. I kept saying to myself over and over again, "I did everything right." I had lost over 100 pounds, I was the healthiest I had been for most of my adult life, and yet I got that phone call. After everything I did, I had to hear the words, "You Have Cancer." Three words no one wants to hear.

As soon as I walked in the house, I barely had to say anything. My family was there, and by the look on my face, they knew I got the results – and that they weren't good. Telling them the news was the hardest thing I had to do after getting the diagnosis. The second hardest thing I had to do was walk across the street to my dad's house and tell him that his daughter has cancer. I was hysterical but, surprisingly, he wasn't. He just hugged me and told me I was going to be ok.

What happened after this first day following the diagnosis is mostly a blur. I think I was so numb from the shock that it's actually hard to remember exactly what I did and felt. I just went to work the next day. Not only did I have to tell my friends, colleagues, and my boss, but I also had to tell my friend who urged me to see my doctor in the first place. It didn't end there. I then had to tell the rest of my family – my sister, brother, uncle, and friends. It was painful every time. Once everybody knew, that's when the work really began. Within a two-week period, I went for four opinions, each with an oncologist and breast surgeon. One of my biggest concerns was that the opinions would all be different but, thankfully, they all had the same treatment and surgical plans for this type of cancer (HER2 +++). About three weeks after the diagnosis, the oncologist who provided the fourth opinion said, "You cannot wait any longer. It's been three weeks. You need to start treatment immediately." She was right. From the time I was diagnosed on October 10, until the time I started treatment on November 9, my tumor had doubled in size. I chose a treatment team and tried to prepare myself for the inevitable next step: chemotherapy ("chemo").

The Treatment Process

Walking into the cancer center for the first time on November 9, 2016, I didn't know what to expect. It was one of the scariest things I've ever faced, wondering how I was going to react to the medication, what it was going to feel like. Was I going to get sick? Was I going to throw up? Would I feel tired all the time? Is my stomach going to be able to handle it? Was it going to hurt? I went to my first chemo treatment, sadly, without my husband. He was away on an important trip with my oldest daughter. It was terrifying to do this for the first time without him, but my youngest daughter and sister were with me. And I got through it. Just like the days following my diagnosis, the first few treatments were a blur. I was still reeling from the diagnosis and trying to cope with the shock of finding myself in a cancer center, as a patient.

At first, the chemo treatments were biweekly. I was able to pick the day I had treatment, which was helpful because I was working full time. Wednesdays were best for me because I would do the treatment, go to work Thursday and Friday, be absolutely exhausted by Friday night, and have the weekend to recover. Then I was back to work on Monday. I certainly needed the rest, as the chemo drugs I was on, Adriamycin (nicknamed the "red devil") and Cytoxan, are incredibly potent. By my second treatment, around Thanksgiving, my hair started to fall out. My entire family was over for Thanksgiving that year. They were pretty stunned to see me with thinning hair, but I couldn't help but make Seinfeld jokes about being bald. I learned quickly that laughter really is the best medicine. That weekend, I had my hairdresser shave my head so at least I was even! By the third treatment, I was completely bald. There was no hair to be found - not on my head, my eyebrows, anywhere.

By January 2017, I was on to the next phase of treatment. I now had a weekly chemo infusion of a different drug, Taxol, which lasted twelve weeks. Starting around this time, I also began infusions of another two drugs, Herceptin and Perjeta, which I received every three weeks through the end of December 2017. Once I started this phase, I had to stop working full time. I started taking half-days on Friday because by midday, I was exhausted. I had no energy, and simply could not get through the day. The Taxol infusions continued through March, and then I had my first of many surgeries on April 24, 2017 – a bilateral mastectomy and removal of three sentinel lymph nodes. During this surgery, the breast reconstructive surgeon came in to put tissue expanders in to prepare my body for the implants I would eventually have. I left the next day in a lot of pain with four drains hanging out of me.

Following the mastectomy, I had multiple reconstructive surgeries. On September 8, 2017, I had the "Exchange Procedure," where the breast reconstructive surgeon removed the tissue expanders and put the implants in. I had textured implants put in, as they were said to have a more "natural" look. On January 8, 2018, I had nipple reconstruction surgery. In order to reconstruct my nipples, the plastic surgeon needed to take skin from somewhere on my body. He suggested taking it from my thighs and that would have left me with more scars. I also needed to have fat injected into the pockets above the implants to make them look more natural. I asked the doctor if he could take the excess skin hanging from my abdomen, which I had as a result of losing over 100 pounds. He said, "Of course! And while I'm at it, I can remove some of the fat cells from your abdomen, too." Again, finding the humor, I told everyone how excited I was that I'd be getting new boobs (that don't sag with age) and a tummy tuck!

After that surgery, I thought this whole terrible ordeal was finally coming to an end. And then I got a letter from my breast reconstructive surgeon saying that the implants I had were recalled due to a link to lymphoma, and that they needed to be replaced. I had this additional surgery on August 10, 2020. It was originally scheduled for April, but was postponed until August due to COVID. This time was such a different experience from the other surgeries. My husband had to drop me off at the front door and couldn't come back until I was ready to be discharged. What an eerie feeling! Just like at the cancer center, everyone at the hospital made me feel like a queen. They were wonderful.

Again, I thought the process was over, but two years later, in the summer of 2022, I was lying down on my right side and felt a pop and tearing feeling in my right armpit. My right implant felt like it moved into my armpit, and then a week later it happened on the left side. My husband and I had moved to South Florida in August 2021, and as excited I was for this new adventure, I was terrified of leaving my oncologist and breast reconstructive surgeon in New York. And this was exactly why. This process never seemed to end. Right away, I called my oncologist in New York who gave me the name of a breast reconstructive surgeon he knew in my area. Unfortunately, this doctor doesn't do revision surgeries. I was given another name and was told the same thing: he doesn't do revision surgeries either. Finally, I was given the name of a breast reconstructive surgeon who does do revisions and was happy to provide a consultation. I guess it's true that the third time's the charm, and I found a wonderful new doctor. Based on his assessment, we'll schedule another surgery to close the pocket that opened up around the implant. I was similarly fortunate enough to find a new oncologist as well. He started his career at the same cancer center I went to in New York, Memorial Sloan Kettering, and he even grew up one town over from me. It felt like it was meant to be.

The World Doesn't Stop Turning When You Get a Cancer Diagnosis

As painstaking as my journey was from diagnosis through surgeries, this was not the only thing going on in our lives at the time. Unfortunately, even when tragedy strikes, the rest of the world continues to move forward. Other things happen, even at times when you think you couldn't possibly handle another obstacle. The year before my diagnosis, we lost my husband's mother very quickly and unexpectedly. Then in 2016, my father-in-law, who was diagnosed with colon cancer in 2014, became very ill, and sadly passed away about two months after my diagnosis. Because I was immunocompromised from the chemo, I had to be very careful in crowds, so I wore a surgical mask to my father-in-law's funeral (pre-COVID!). Then, at the end of the year, my oldest daughter left for vet school in the Caribbean.

Because I didn't have the power to change any of these occurrences, I knew the only thing I could do was to keep pushing forward. I wanted to keep things as normal as possible during this time. I continued to work as a nursing school lab instructor, volunteered as an EMT, and worked out at my bootcamp classes a few times a week when I had enough energy. Keeping my routines and sense of normalcy helped me to focus on what I could do, instead of dwelling on what I couldn't. This wasn't always easy. Keeping up with the "hustle and bustle" of life is hard even on our best days, but it can be nearly impossible when we're struggling with a serious illness or other kind of crisis. I learned this as I tried to continue working during my chemo treatments and surgeries. Not everyone understood the day-to-day challenges I was facing, and didn't know how to handle the situation. For instance, I was scrutinized and questioned for having to leave work early when I wasn't feeling well or when I needed to take more time off for another surgery. I would get comments from supervisors like "We're short-staffed. You'll have to figure it out" and "Oh, another surgery? Well, at least it's not cancer." It was hard enough to mentally and physically get through this time in my life, and to be made to feel like I was doing something wrong by taking care of myself was incomprehensible.

But this often happens to people. Not everyone is shown the love and compassion they should. I was just grateful that this was only an issue at work. I had unending support from my family, friends, and neighbors. They were with me every step of the way. My sister traveled from out of state to keep me company at nearly all of my chemo treatments, along with my youngest daughter, and my husband came with me to all of my doctor appointments and surgeries. Neighbors brought meals and offered to do laundry. Even the students at work provided love and support during this time. Accepting this much help from people was very hard for me. I was the one to care for others. I'm the nurse. I'm the EMT. It was challenging to not be in that role.

Learning to Accept Support

An incredibly important lesson I learned during all of this was that I was allowed to accept help. It didn't change who I was. I was always the caretaker, but that didn't mean I would be judged for being the one who needed care. I was truly afraid of not being loved and being judged by others because I had to take care of myself first and not feel guilty about it. That fear paralyzed me in a way that is not understood by many people. In those moments, I felt like I was five years old again, getting teased for being different, not feeling loved. I was such a sensitive child, ready to cry at a moment's notice. Those feelings came full circle at a time when my life was being turned upside down. Through this, I learned that it was okay to put myself first, without guilt or judgment or pressure. Not being the caretaker this time didn't mean

I was never going to be the caretaker again. I just couldn't take care of everyone and everything during this time –I needed to get better first. I came to realize that none of this defined me. Not the diagnosis, not the fact that I needed help. I was still me. I was still a mom, wife, daughter, sister, nurse, and EMT. And I was going to beat this.

People often ask me what kept me going through the treatments and surgeries, which is actually a hard question to answer. I don't know if it was luck, perseverance, or love that got me through it. It was probably all three. Every day I just tried my best to find the positive and keep busy with my normal routine. I refused to let this illness change my story without my permission. Anyone who knows me will tell you I'm stubborn. My first reaction to someone telling me I can't do something or that I'm not good enough is, "Watch me." And my cancer journey was no different. I was told I had a fatal disease. Well, I wasn't going to let it be fatal. And of course it is easy to say this now – there certainly were better days than others – and I would tell myself not to dwell on it. Each day I would just pick up where I left off, continuing to fight. And it's gotten me to where I am today – Happy, Healthy, and Loved!

Dina Legland

Dina Legland is a Certified Life and Wellness Coach who uses her personal and professional experience to help clients conquer their fears to achieve a lifestyle filled with joy, freedom, and inner peace. As the founder of Wellness Warriors for Life, LLC, Dina is a Wellness Warrior, Registered Nurse, and EMT for over 30 years.

Dina spent her professional life taking care of others by treating home care patients as a field nurse, children as a public-school nurse, and as a home care agency director. She exemplifies what it means to be a strong, courageous leader in the community. Helping others is simply a part of who she is.

As the Inner Warrior Coach, she educates people to face their greatest fears, transforming them into being empowered and confident. Dina is uniquely qualified to support others to release their fears given her own personal struggles with debilitating fears and how she overcame and mastered it. As a cancer survivor and thrivor, Dina always says, "Cancer Saved My Life, and My Fears Almost Killed Me!" Her journey and experience of battling and being victorious have contributed to her passion and purpose. Her mission is to share her experiences, wisdom, tools, strategies, and humor to conquer uncontrollable fears and to seek inner wellness with freedom guilt-free.

When not working with clients, you can find Dina on podcasts and speaking to organizations around the world. She loves exploring nature trails, dancing to live music, walking on the beach, and tasting wine at vineyards with her husband of 34+ years and two daughters.

Connect with Dina at www.wellnesswarriorsforlife.com.

CHAPTER 5

Together We Can Do Anything

Jess Riney

"You've got this, you just don't know it yet," said a friend of mine in the initial days of my cancer diagnosis. This inspirational phrase can encourage anyone to overcome a challenge, and I believe it transcends this lifetime.

On January 6th, 2021, as our country's freedom seemed to hang in the balance on insurrection day, a part of my life ended. Not long ago someone asked me, "Do you remember when you were diagnosed with your cancer?" Later I thought, "how can you forget?" So much of that day is etched in my memory. It was late afternoon and the hospital's phone number appeared on my cell phone screen. I remember pacing around the house with my mind reeling, attempting to keep my composure, trying to ask good questions and get an idea of what to expect moving forward. One in eight women received the same news I did. I thought, why not me? The nurse on the phone was amazing. She told me, "You are going to go through some hard things, but you are going to be okay." After the phone call, I broke the news to my wife. It took her breath away. We received my results the day after my biopsy, and no one was expecting the news to come that quickly. Next, I called my mom. I needed her with me. Then we drove across town to tell my twin sister and her wife. Along the way, I talked to my brother and sister-in-law. The following day I called and talked to more family. I wanted them to hear the news from me. I shared my raw emotion, but I was bringing together our "team." I knew we would get through this because we had each other. Our family mantra quickly became, "Teamwork makes the dream work."

A cancer diagnosis and subsequent treatment is truly a roller coaster. From the initial investigation to the results being relayed, "There was a significant finding from your biopsy, you have invasive ductal carcinoma." Then came the parade of doctors' appointments and additional scans scheduled (cancer units are certainly well-oiled machines, a testament to the many patients that grace their floors). Finally, after a frightening number of days, I was given my prognosis and treatment plan. So now I knew what I was up against and what to focus on.

I invested my natural strengths (positivity, hard work, being a planner, and adaptability) to fight my cancer. All I had to do was look at my beautiful, amazing, precious children to know I would do anything to have more time with them. What I learned along the way helped shape my character more. I learned to give grace, be more patient with others, to focus on what's in our control, to slow down and live in the moment, to accept vulnerabilities, and to ask for help.

After I allowed some time for my diagnosis to sink in and before I began treatments, I shared on social media what was going on. I asked for our friends and extended family to keep us in their hearts and prayers as we embarked on this whirlwind of a journey. The response was uplifting. As the isolation of the covid pandemic ensued, the virtual or long distant support of others helped us overcome the grueling treatments. For example, when I was struggling or starting a new phase, I asked for motivation in the form of inspirational quotes, "fight" songs, and summer bucket list ideas. Sharing my story on social media was also an opportunity for me to utilize my circumstances to raise awareness and encourage people to keep their checkups/scans and to be mindful of their body. I also used that platform to express gratitude and to thank all the people providing me with emotional, physical, and medical support.

Early detection is certainly a key factor to survivorship. For that I am forever grateful for my gynecologist. I was in for a routine annual exam when my doctor discovered my breast lump. She was hoping it was just my fibrously dense breast tissue. But she wanted it further evaluated, so I was scheduled for a mammogram and diagnostic ultrasound. Being only 36 years old at the time and with no family history of breast cancer, I was too young for a mammogram as part of my regular health plan. I did self-breast exams on occasion, certainly not as frequently or diligently as I should have. I am much more diligent now, but challenges remain in feeling confident in what's going on with my breast tissue, especially after all the impacts to my body, from chemotherapy, surgery, and radiation. There's also a fear to surveillance. What if I find something? It is frightening to think of going through it all again. But I challenge that way of thinking by telling myself, what if you don't find something? What if something is there, and I had the chance to find it, but I didn't, and it moved further throughout my body. I am my first line of defense, so I am going to do all that I can, to continue doing my best.

To give myself the best chance at success during treatment, I utilized the resources available to me, such as entering a program offered through my insurance to talk with a Nurse Care Manager once a month to discuss my health status, treatment approach, medications, and any questions or concerns I had through the process. This was a vital component in preparing me for what was to happen and helped me be a good advocate for myself. I also received counseling services and from that learned to put an imaginary stop sign on my forehead when various anxious thoughts raced through my mind. I joined a breast cancer support group through a local hospital. The connection I feel to the other women and their stories is both emotional and comforting. Various educational opportunities were presented to the group, which helped me better understand a variety of cancer treatments and the potential long-term effects/remedies.

I remember I was just sort of present, and I lacked energy. My strength was reading stories and cuddling the kids, so we did a lot of that. I ate what I could, but meals were anxiety provoking because I knew I needed to eat but nothing tasted right, and my appetite was low. I remember at times the kids gravitated towards their momma, Crystal. At just 5 1/2 and 3 years old, they could tell my strength was waning. Crystal was the anchor all of us needed. Because of these memories, now when our daughter leaps into my arms when I pick her up from preschool, and when our son holds my hand and says he always will, I smile bigger and hold on more dearly because I know the fragility of those moments. At one point during my chemotherapy, I was so sick from a mild case of pneumonia and a clot in my port that I had two emergency room visits in a week, one by ambulance (my first ambulance experience). From that day on and every day since, we do nighttime family hugs.

The most challenging part of my treatment was the chemotherapy. My doctors told me whatever my side effects were after the first round I would likely experience for the rest of my treatment (six rounds to completion of the hard stuff, which took about four months). What I did not realize was how much my body would deteriorate by then. I wished to be done after round four, but I tried to focus on the importance of allowing the chemotherapy to do its job, kill all the cancer cells. I prayed it would leave the rest of me intact. I knew if I struggled to keep going, my sister would be there to push or pull me along. She was so focused on my battle. Being identical twins, I think she could feel my experience on a different level than the rest of my family. I often called her my secret weapon. My cancer did not know it was being battled by both of us.

My final round of chemotherapy was truly a feat to climb. I was unable to eat much more than vanilla ice-cream for about a week. That brought on our second family mantra "Just be held." I remember falling into my family's arms. One day I was lying in bed, crying, and my mom laid with me, holding me.

There are things I wish I could forget (please keep in mind these were some of my personal hardships; everyone has their own experience/side effects from treatments): coughing up blood clots from significant nose bleeds and subsequent nose cauterizations; feeling tingly all over like I could feel my cells bursting; fluttering heartbeats; my pale bald reflection when I looked my worst; puffy cheeks from blocked salivary ducts; how the taste of food I usually loved was not appetizing at all; the many fears, for example fearing being outside in the cold weather because I knew my body would not be able to fight off a slight infection; the infusaport in my chest wall; my drain bag after surgery; having to walk into the radiation treatment room with nothing on from the waist up every day for four straight weeks; the stress my cancer put on our whole family; the anxiety my son felt and attempting to reassure him when he was upset at night, wanting me to cuddle him, because he was afraid I was going to die (a helpful book we read together was *Becky and the Worry Cup: A Children's Book About a Parent's Cancer* by Wendy S. Harpham).

But most of all, there are things I hope I never forget. It is all about perspective. If you can adjust to look at things with a new "lens," then the challenges you face are lessons to be learned. I hope I can utilize my experience to help make other people's journeys a little easier. For example, here's some good advice I learned: 1) when you "hit a wall," it is there for you to rest upon; 2) do not rush out of the moments (even the hard ones), allow yourself to feel it all and be patient; and 3) do your best to embrace the vulnerability of your experience, allowing others to help build you up. I was able to truly focus on the here and now and appreciate watching my family. I watched as they played in the snow in the winter and then plant flowers in the spring. I watched them knowing I would eventually be thriving again instead of fighting to survive. I would return an active participant in their lives, hopefully an improved version of myself. My cancer gave me the opportunity to show my kids how to overcome something extremely challenging.

One of the most challenging parts of my journey (certainly the most heartbreaking) was losing my dearest grandma. I was very close with her, and she was a huge support for our family in various life circumstances. During my cancer treatment, she wrote to me saying she wished she could take this for me. She wanted me to have the long, amazing life that she had. The day after my last round of chemotherapy, I had an MRI to see how my cancer had responded. The results indicated a complete response. The chemotherapy worked. I had no more invasive cancer cells! Tragically, not even a week later, we found out my grandma had an aggressive brain cancer and it would take her within a couple of months. My heart shattered. The pain of her loss felt greater than the cancer treatments I was undergoing. I was grateful I was able to be with her, to hold her, to say goodbye. I still struggle with her not being here. But I know she will be the first arms I leap into when it is my turn to cross heaven's gates.

At one time I thought, "Please, God, help me get to at least when the kids are a bit older, and they do not need me as much." Then I realized that time will never come. I know my children will always need me. The way in which they do will change, just like I need my grandma, and she's still here in spirit. Eventually we all live on within the hearts of our loved ones. Until then, all you can do is keep on keeping on, making the best memories possible or being patient for when you are thriving once again.

When I think about the "me" at the beginning of my treatment and the "me" now, there aren't too many differences that can be depicted from a glance. When you look a bit closer, however, you may see a few more scars, some swelling, decay, chronic fatigue, and brain fog. If you look a bit deeper, you might see someone with more hope, love, passion, and peace. Of course, just like most things in life, personal growth does not happen in a straight upward line. It is more of a zig zag. There are days I feel lost, broken, and weary. Other times I feel prepared and strong. A quote I often turn to is this: "You can handle anything, because you've already handled everything." ~ from *A Boy Called Christmas*. That's a life lesson I want our kids to take from 2021, the lesson that sometimes you get knocked down, and that's okay, we get back up (by the help of others), brush ourselves off, and keep on trekking.

Being a year into remission, I continue to learn and adapt to being a cancer survivor. I imagine most survivors can resonate with the quote "you have to be willing to die in order to truly live" (Raven Reyes, 'The 100'). Cancer treatments kill off parts of you in order to save the rest of you; it is a double-edged sword. The treatments target the cancer, but there can be residual damage along the way. During treatment I had an autoimmune disease flare up, moderate tooth decay, and was diagnosed with lymphedema (an incurable but manageable condition caused by blockage in the lymphatic system, which drains fluid from our bodies, often a result of cancer treatments). These are some continued challenges I face, but I would do it all again for the priceless opportunity of more time. So, for the cancer survivors out there, I feel you. I know the guilt you carry, even though this was not a path we chose, but fell upon us. For the many more caregivers out there I want you to know I see you. You did have a choice; you chose to stick around for the hard. I see you at the doctors' appointments. I know through what I have seen in my own caregivers what sacrifices you make and the fears you bury. There is so much vulnerability to needing caregivers. For me, as a stay-at-home parent, there were no "sick days." I required help to make sure our kids were taken care of, and their lives continued to be enriched despite our circumstances. So, I also see the beauty in it. Caregiving is a testament of true love. For example, true love is bringing your spouse their pills and a drink of water to bed so they can fall right back to sleep after taking morning medication. It is staying up for late-night soul-searching conversations. It is changing out drain bags after surgery. It is doing all the things in between with two feet in, steady strength, and no complaints. It is a sister taking off a week from work to help after surgery instead of having a true vacation to recharge from a challenging career. It is a mom juggling caregiving for her dying mother while still trying to support her daughter and family through a major challenge. It is a brother and sister-in-law moving in for a week and throwing a party for a 3-year-old when everything seemed to be crashing down. The role of caregivers is absolutely everything!!

Currently I am focused on living life with a balance of reality that my aggressive cancer can return anytime, but not to fear it. Instead, use it as motivation to live more boldly and love bigger. Such as the Latin phrase *Dulcius Ex Asperis*, which translates to "sweeter after difficulties" (quoted by Sandra Bullock in the movie 'The Lost City'). In some ways my cancer set me free. Gaining a better understanding of the fragility of life has pushed me to not hold back on doing things outside of my comfort zone, on telling those I love how I feel, or fighting for things I believe in. It has also taught me how to let go of negativity, unrealistic expectations, and unnecessary worry. I am also more focused on experiences. When I think about putting money or energy into something, I think about what type of memories we can make.

In the next chapter of my life, I want to focus on embracing life with my family and giving back. I want to reflect on the hard things we have overcome and be reminded that together we can do anything (something my grandma often said). I also want to share my story in hopes it can help other families in some small way. I want to be a support to others going through a similar challenge. I really believe we are stronger together. By working together to combat cancer, we are also honoring the lives of everyone who has battled and brawled and is a cherished memory. We are honoring families who have endured and sacrificed so much to help honor lives forever changed because of a complex powerful word, while fearlessly searching for tomorrow's cures. So, remember, "you've got this," even if you don't know it quite yet.

Jess Riney

Jess Riney is a 38-year-old stay-at-home mom from Springfield, Illinois. She met her wife, Crystal, while attending college. They have been married 11 years and have two children, Jaxon and Maya (7 1/2 & 5 years old). Jess is a wife, mother, sister, daughter, friend, and cancer survivor.

In January 2021, she was diagnosed with Stage 1 HER2+ invasive ductal carcinoma. She underwent six rounds of hard chemotherapy, had a lumpectomy, completed four weeks of radiation, and three-week infusions for the entire year to help reduce chances of reoccurrence. Jess is currently considered "in remission."

She hopes to eventually be cancer free and live a long, full life, but is preparing herself in case her cancer returns. No matter what the future holds, she wants cancer to inspire her to love bigger and live more boldly. Jess soaks up her days playing at home, exploring the outdoors, visiting with family, and going on little getaways. She looks forward to making more memories: dancing in the living room, watching sunsets at the hill, backyard bonfires, swimming, bike riding, sledding, playdates with friends, family get-togethers, and road trips in the family van. Jess is a motivator and enjoys cheering on her children as they participate in various extracurricular activities. She is excited to see what passions they find as they continue to venture through life.

Connect with Jess at https://www.facebook.com/jessica.f.riney.

CHAPTER 6

A Tragic Journey Full of Blessings

Lauren Engelke-Smith

A positive mind is not just in the mind. It requires incorporating positive people, activities, and things into your life that bring on these positive feelings. ~Lauren Marie Engelke-Smith

"Get back to your room! We think you have leukemia," the doctor said running down the hallway as she met the nurse pushing me downstairs to meet my husband in the car to go home after about a week stay in the hospital while they were doing tests. What a surprise, I thought, then shock and crying overwhelmed me as I was frantically calling my husband to come back upstairs while nurses and doctors flooded my room in scrubs and lab coats. This would become my new normal.

New normal? What is it? I still don't even know and I'm 180+ days after transplant. I spent forty-six days in a dreaded, bland, stark white hospital room with all of its annoying beeps, lights, and sounds. As the heat of July in 2021 whittled away outside, I was only allowed to see my kids one time before I started the 7-3 chemo regimen. However, I had two rules during that time.

DO NOT read any literature about AML and stay positive! I did not want to know what I was about to go through and yes, I knew a few people that had AML, but not many and I did not know their treatment plan or what they went through. I just knew that it is different for everyone.

How can you stay positive without knowing what to expect? God. Over the next few weeks school started for my three kids ages seventeen, twelve, and nine. This was their first real school year since we moved during covid in 2020 to a new house and new school district. Luckily God knew what was coming and knew I would be sick because I ordered their school supplies through a school fundraiser the prior school year and all my husband had to do was stick it in a book bag that I had already bought. Everything was labeled with their names. Now who could have predicted that I would be sick and be done school shopping on July 22nd for the upcoming school year? That's never happened before. There are many other ways that I stayed positive throughout this journey and God has used so many people to help me stay positive.

My daughter

The night before I was diagnosed, I took a bath in our "chakuzi" (as my nine-year-old calls it) and I developed red spots all over my body. I thought the water was too hot and didn't really think anything of it, but showed my husband. My seventeen-year-old daughter, who is never sick, came into our room at 12:30am crying that her ear hurt. My husband said to take her to prompt care in the morning to get medicine and to have the doctor look at the spots on me. The doctor ended up taking a blood test and by noon they called me to let me know my platelets were 11,000 (150,000 is normal) and to get to a hospital now since I could bleed to death. That was the start of my forty-six-day hospital stay and my last day of work as an Assistant Principal. I was transferring to a new job closer to home, but I never got to teach. Our daughter watched our two sons when my husband would be visiting with me or while he was away with me as my caregiver during my stem cell transplant. She did laundry, dishes, kept the house straight, and continued to make the honor roll in AP and had dual credit classes in high school. I am so proud of how she stepped up and helped us all. I am most grateful my daughter saved my life. Where in your journey have coincidences happened and things have worked out when you least expected it?

My husband

Other than not liking to put away laundry, there isn't much my husband doesn't do. He's a great guy and has supported me through my bachelors, masters, and Special Education, Early Childhood, and School Administration certifications. He put lotion all over me when my body began to peel from head to toe after the transplant. He holds my hand when we are walking out and about. I was bedridden for a few days and he had to actually wipe my butt after a very high temperature landed me in intermediate care under a frozen blanket. (Some things didn't wait for old age.) I hope anyone going through this has been given someone like my husband. Think about who your person is and thank them.

My in-laws and my mom

With me not working, we had to cut our budget in half. That isn't exactly easy when gas prices are up to almost $6.00 and food costs have gone up at least 15% in some cases. Basically, my husband's salary covers our bills and anything else has come from food and house supplies from my in-laws, food pantries, gift cards, church, neighbors, other family, and small cancer foundation checks to cover co-pays and prescriptions. God always provides material things when the need is great.

My friends and family

At one point during my first stay in the hospital, I was updating up to forty-six people per day on my progress as it was a shock to all of us. I was kept very busy with these updates and it was great to connect with my church friends, friends from back home in Maryland and Delaware, and family across the United States. I would get cards in the mail nearly every day and display them on my card can (you know the old fashion ones that are made with yarn and a coffee can?). My friend still texts me Bible verses every day. When I was in the hospital, I would write them on paper and tape them to my wall, but then I had to move rooms and that was a pain to take off. The nurses had a heck of a time with all that tape. To keep my thoughts positive and mind busy, I would also send homemade cards to my friends. That was one thing that I enjoyed doing when I was little. I would make cards for every family member each Christmas. They weren't super fancy, but it was special to personalize each one. One day during my first stay in the hospital my nurse and a mutual friend said, "You have got to meet ____." The patient ended up being a couple of doors down from my room and had the same diagnosis.

God again stepped up to connect us and we talked when we felt good enough to visit. We were sent home to prepare for our stem cell transplants which were scheduled within a day of each other at the same hospital, same floor. We ended up walking miles together around the floor to keep our energy up and in twenty-five days I walked twenty-five miles. We were both out of there within three weeks, which is unheard of in the stem cell recovery plan. Usually, you are in the hospital for three months. I am glad I have her to talk to. Even though our journeys are different, they are similar.

Support has also come from other family members who have sent funds to help us with food and other expenses and we are so thankful for all the prayers that were sent up on my behalf. I learned that you can't have flowers in your room if you are going through chemo because of the bacteria that might be on them. That was new to me. Besides sending flowers to cancer patients, what would you do for friends or family in a difficult time in their life?

My donor

A twenty-nine-year-old male from somewhere in the United States saved my life on my re-birthday, December 13, 2021. Eight years prior to my transplant, our son had a bone marrow transplant because he was born with a rare form of anemia, so we were familiar with the preparation, process, and after-care that was needed. However, my team did not tell me ALL of the effects of the transplant during and after. Our son recovered very quickly and had no side effects except cataracts due to high doses of steroids. So, I thought my recovery would be similar and therefore I wasn't worried about the transplant. I haven't had serious issues, just little skin and respiratory issues. While I was in the hospital, I'm grateful to have only had one fever and was only on IV nutrition for a couple of days because I could not swallow. My son met his donor who was a 19-year-old from Germany when Make-a-Wish granted his wish, and we all got to thank him for saving his life. I can't wait to meet my donor if he approves to meet me. Who would you like to thank for significantly changing or saving your life? What would you say to them? (I was crying too hard the whole week when we met my son's donor, but I finally got the words out.)

Keeping busy

When I first came home from the hospital, I was always cold so I sat on the couch a lot with my heated blanket and with my dog, Skylar. That was therapy. But then the daily check-ins from friends and family dwindled as I transferred updates to one social media post after doctor appointments and I became bored.

As the school year came to an end, my three kids were now home. They keep me busy. I'm a teacher and what do all teachers do during summer? That's right, make their kids learn. (Maybe not all teachers do that, but I do.) I'm utilizing free programs the library and community offer since our funds are still low until I can work next school year. I am part of an educational book study about reading curriculums in the United States. I have made it a point to meet a friend for lunch once a week because we all need friend time. I call a different relative each day of the week. I have prepared my classroom decor for next school year and talked to some wonderful teachers I met from the district. Our friends have opened their pools and let us chill out. I love to cook, so finding new recipes has become a hobby; however, "chemo brain" is a real thing and remembering more than one step of a recipe is difficult. I end up looking at my recipe 100 times in order to remember the next step. I've been reviewing my Dyslexia materials so I can go back to tutoring students with dyslexia. I still send cards to people, especially when I see birthday posts of strangers on my social media. My kids, husband, and I take the dog on walks. God has given me plenty to do! What positive things do you do to keep busy?

After telling my story, can you see God strategically moving parts around like on a chess board? Throughout my journey, I have had several reminders that He is next to me every step of the way. Like today, while writing this, my husband brought me a check for $500 from a cancer foundation grant that someone must have applied for on my behalf. Thank God because we are almost out of money until my husband gets paid. Things like this always happen when we least expect it.

As I'm reviewing this chapter to submit it for publishing, I'm waiting on my twelve-year-old's bone marrow biopsy results. You heard that right … now he's going to have to get a bone marrow transplant. Life happens and can change in a split second. Just today I thought, "I can be gone tomorrow. I could have died last summer. Since I didn't, every day is an awesome day and I need to pass on the positives wherever I go." Whether it's Aplastic Anemia, Bone Marrow Failure, or leukemia like our family has dealt with or you are just having a bad day, promise me that you will stay positive and look for God in every step.

Lauren Engelke-Smith

Lauren Engelke-Smith is 44 years old. She was born in Maryland and relocated to Illinois in 2003 with her husband, Aaron.

She is most importantly a mom of 3 kids, special educator, aspiring school administrator, and dyslexia tutor. Lauren's leukemia journey is just one of many tragedies her family has been through that has led to infinite blessings.

Connect with Lauren at

https://www.facebook.com/lauren.engelkesmith.

CHAPTER 7

Check Your Boobs, Mine Tried to Kill Me

Lisa Woods

Have you ever been asked if you survived? I have and, spoiler alert, I did. The June after I completed chemo, I was shopping for outdoor flowers. Upon returning to my car, I noticed the one parked next to me was the same make, color, and similar model to mine. By the time I unloaded, returned my cart, and headed back, the owner was there unlocking his vehicle. I spoke out, "Hey, I like your car." He smiled, then realized why I said that. My car, being the sport model, had options that his did not. He began pointing out things on my sedan that he wished his car had, like the spoiler and the V6 engine. Then he noticed the sticker on the window and said, "And yours has boobs." It's just the word, not a picture, but it's the largest word. I read the sticker out loud, "Check your boobs, mine tried to kill me," and said it was because I had had breast cancer. He replied, "I'm sorry, did you survive?" I responded in the affirmative and told him I had recently had reconstructive surgery. He said it appeared the doctor had done a fine job. I thanked him, got in my car, and sat there laughing. The whole thing was comical.

I answered yes to the question of whether or not I was alive. A friend suggested that I should have told him I survived but my boobs didn't. I was too stunned to think that quickly. I know that he likely meant to ask if I was going to be okay; that question had come up before. He was taken aback by my matter-of-fact statement about having breast cancer and it came out wrong. I'm an expert in not saying things the way I mean them, so no judgment here. He probably got in his car wondering what in the hell had just happened. I hope he laughed, too.

You may wonder why I even initiated that conversation. Well, it was a beautiful day, I was feeling good, I was alive and happy to be so. I wanted to share a smile and some humanity, and it turned out greater than I could have imagined. Small, unplanned interactions like that add spice to life, and when they result in amusement, even better. Laughter may not be the best medicine, actual medicine is vitally important, but it is definitely healing. Finding merriment and the silver lining in trying situations is what helps me get through them with the least amount of damage. That definitely helped me manage my way through breast cancer. I'm not saying that there's anything funny about cancer, because there is not, but just like in everyday life, there will be humor in some of the situations you run into. Grab the joy from those and save it for later.

I was the seventh woman in my family to receive a breast cancer diagnosis. It is a big, beautiful, wonderful family full of amazing people who would go to the ends of the earth to help any member. I am also fortunate to have found that I had more friends and support than I was even aware. I don't take any of that for granted and I will be forever grateful to each person who stepped up for me and will hold certain events in my heart eternally. As much as I appreciate everyone in those categories, it is not a surprise to get assistance from those in your camp. What was surprising and strengthened my faith in society were the blessings of advice, encouragement, and random acts of kindness from strangers and the opportunity to return the same to others. I navigated my cancer by being candid about having it and willing to talk with others about it. That willingness opened me up to receive those blessings. Every interaction is an important piece of my story.

As I mentioned, I wasn't the first in the family to face the pink nightmare that is breast cancer. My mom is a two-time survivor, in addition, my grandmother, three aunts and a great-aunt were also part of the club. I was not surprised to be handed my diagnosis; I had expected it for nearly twenty years before it happened. I thought I was prepared, and in some respects I was. I knew it could be dealt with, I watched my mom do it twice and move on with her life. The initial shock was short lived, and I didn't experience the *why me* phase that many do. At least I didn't question why it happened to me, but rather what I was supposed to do with it. Instead, I put on my brave girl wings, straightened my tiara, and forged straight ahead into surgery and treatment with strength and determination. I was going to face it, fight it, conquer it, and come out the other side with little to no interruption to my life. Are you kidding? What was I thinking?

Chemo was never a part of my plan, but we all know that the best-laid plans often go awry. My cancer was caught early at stage I. I should have been able to have surgery, reconstruction and then finish it off with five years of Tamoxifen to afford the best chance of it not coming back. I could have done that, but a grade III, HER2+ addition to the tumor pathology made it an aggressive triple-positive enemy whose best treatment option runs alongside chemotherapy. That changed everything. The strong, brave, stubborn, independent woman who was going to show cancer her middle finger, was knocked slightly off balance. I was still worthy of all of those great adjectives; I was just a bit less sure of myself. As I progressed through chemo, I was, at times, truly scared of what was happening to my body and had to acknowledge that the whole thing really was about a sometime killer that I had taken for granted. Like I said, it was caught early, and I was doing everything advised to keep it away in the future. I had total faith in my medical teams and complete faith in God to be with me and walk me through the fire as He had done so many times before; however, fear of the unknown can still creep in and take root. I talked with my doctors and searched online for all the information I could glean about the possible lasting or future effects of chemotherapy, the probability of cancer recurrence, life expectancy with my type of cancer and treatment plan, etc. I craved a good look at my potential future outcome. Doctors can give you percentages and odds, but those still leave ample room for luck. Of course, those numbers are used to determine medical interventions, but they relegate much of what your after-treatment life will be to the imagination. The prominent information on the internet is also based on the same statistics focusing on the five or ten-year survival rates after treatment. There is so much info out there that it can be difficult to sort through and extract what you are truly looking for. You also have to be careful of the doom and gloom scenarios lurking around every corner in the online space. I yearned for real world examples of long-term survivors who were treated with the same poison I was subjecting myself to. I needed to see that they were out there thriving more than five or ten years later. Ask and you shall receive.

It was a Friday in October after my third treatment when I was brought to tears in the checkout lane of my local grocery store. I was feeling terrible but needed a couple of essentials at that point: toilet paper and Doritos. Chemo was playing games with my bowels, so it was imperative to keep an abundance of free rolling TP on hand at all times. Thanks to the Carboplatin infusions, most food tasted like metal. The delicious snack chips covered in heavy cheddar cheese dust were one of the few items that my tastebuds enjoyed and made me want to eat. I entered treatment with a plan to consume only healthy foods, not knowing that they would soon mostly taste like literal trash. A fellow cancer survivor clued me in on finding flavorful foods to overpower the industrial taste; Doritos did that successfully. I was a week out from the most recent chemo treatment and was feeling awful. I dragged myself into the store that night only because I needed those things to make it through the weekend. It was getting late, and the store was quiet. I took my goodies and randomly chose an open checkout lane. As I set my purchases down on the belt, I was greeted with a smile and questions about how I was doing and if I had found everything all right. I was wearing a t-shirt with a pink ribbon on it, a jacket with a pink ribbon on it and my bald head was covered with a scarf adorned with little pink ribbons. I was teetering on the verge of tears because of feeling so miserable but I answered that I was okay, not true, and that I had found what I needed, true. I know the clerk saw through my forced smile. He asked if I was a survivor. I told him that I was in the middle of it and currently going through chemo. He said he felt for me and knew what it was like, then proceeded to tell me his story.

Nineteen years earlier, Doctors had diagnosed him with Non-Hodgkin's Lymphoma. He endured twenty rounds of chemo and radiation to put it into remission. A couple of years later it returned, and he underwent a stem cell transplant. It was tough and he questioned why him, but he made it through and was in good health. He told me to keep going and I would get through it. He said he would pray for me, and I believe that night that he did. I paid for my groceries and thanked him through watery eyes. That encounter certainly put things in a different light for me. I was questioning chemo at that point and tired of feeling sick. That man renewed my determination. If he could tolerate all of that, I could certainly face what I had left.

I believe I will always remember that grocery clerk. I was directed to his line because I needed that interaction, a shot of perspective. He didn't have to open up and tell me something so personal, but he could see that I was down and would benefit from it. I have endeavored to extend the same to others when I can see it is needed. We are all just human and being human is hard, some times are harder than others. In those extra tough periods, a few kind words of encouragement can make that which is unpleasant more tolerable; often times, they can even change your entire outlook. I would continue to see that cashier down at the store, always smiling and friendly. Six years after our meeting, I mentioned our conversation to him and inquired about his health. He was still doing well, and I let him know that I was, too. I thanked him again for speaking up that night, it helped renew my spirit. I am a firm believer that God drops the right people into our lives at the right times and puts us where He needs us to be when He needs us to be there. I have had this happen too many times to merely be coincidence.

About two months later, that timing struck again. It was the week before Christmas, and I had one chemo treatment left. I was toying with the idea of not doing it. I was over it and my fight was wavering. I was struggling with worsening side effects and doubting the *preventative* chemotherapy that I had agreed to do in order to onboard the treatment for the HER2+ component of my cancer. I was worried about the damage it was doing to my body and what the permanence might be. I had done much reading of survivor stories and searching for info on life after chemo, but those people weren't too far out from it; I wasn't finding answers about long-term recovery. I had dropped my boys off at the mall and went to a store across the street to wander around and be out of their vicinity while they shopped. I was wearing a cute hot pink winter cap with a small brim. As a woman was passing by, she told me she liked my hat. I smiled, thanked her, and went on. A little later, we came side by side in an aisle and she stopped again to tell me how much she liked my hat. She said that I really looked nice in it, and she wished that she looked good in hats, but didn't feel like she did. While we stood there talking, she must have noticed that there was a lack of hair sticking out from under my cap in any direction. She suddenly inquired if I needed to wear a hat. I told her I was going through chemo. She asked where I was in treatment, and I relayed that I had just one left. She said she could relate as she had been through it herself.

Twenty-nine years earlier, she had breast, uterine and lung cancer all at the same time. She was an attractive woman who looked to be somewhere in her sixties and healthy. When she told me that, my eyes welled up and I just said, "God bless you!" What a huge burden to face. I asked if the things she lost during chemotherapy had come back for her. She said everything returned except for her eyebrows. There was no numbness, her taste was restored, and she had no other lasting effects from treatment. Her name was Ruth, and she was doing well all those years later. It was a matter of a few moments of conversation, but it was just what I needed. As we parted ways, my worries had been lessened. You never know when an angel in human form is going to drop into your life. Some are meant to be there for a moment and others to stay by your side. Be grateful for each of them.

With my family history, I anticipated a cancer diagnosis, but still hoped that I would dodge the bullet, as it were. When that didn't happen, I embraced my reality and went about deciphering why I had been chosen for the experience and what lessons I should take from it for myself and to share with others. I have learned much that I attempt, though still sometimes fail, to reflect in my daily life. Perspective, patience and attitude are stand outs from my time as a cancer patient and now survivor.

When an annoyance arises, I strive to run it through my *grand scheme of things* test where I weigh how much it truly matters in the grand scheme of things, then proceed accordingly. This is a terrific way to eliminate undue stress. There are often bigger things out there than some of the petty ones we come up against and there is nearly always someone who is facing a larger hardship than you. That is not to imply that what you may be facing is any less important, everyone's stuff is their stuff and it's big when you're on the inside of it, however, perspective can be enlightening.

Having been in situations that required extra patience to be given to me, I also try to afford more grace to those around me. I know what it's like to be cautious and slow moving, so I allow some space in that to others and help them if I can. My newfound grace does not yet extend to driving, but I continue to work on that. Attitude is also of the utmost importance when going through cancer or any major struggle. The way that you face an obstacle often determines whether you conquer it, or it conquers you. Approach it with the desire to be the conqueror.

A strong will may carry you far, but you should not feel the need to shoulder a burden alone. When you open yourself up to others, you make it possible to receive gifts of love, laughter, hope and encouragement that can power your strength and conviction. Lean on your family and friends, draw comfort and courage from your faith and never underestimate the value of your fellow humans. Do not be afraid to put your struggles out there. There may be someone right in front of you who can relate and has just the words that you need to hear or maybe they need to hear from you. Be on the lookout, a random interaction may change your life. It could be a man in a parking lot whose fumbled words brighten your day and make you laugh. It might be a grocery clerk who gives you the nudge you need to rekindle your fighting spirit. It may be a fellow shopper who admires your hat and gives you hope for three decades of cancer survivorship and a body that makes a close return to its original state. It could be a sweet waitress who covers your check for celebratory pie after your final chemo treatment. Or perhaps it will be a survivor who wrote some words in a book and told you that you are stronger than you know, and you are not alone, because I'm out here somewhere rooting for you in honor of those who rooted for me.

Lisa Woods

Lisa Woods is a survivor who turned her breast cancer experience into a captivating literary debut. *When Good Boobs Go Bad; Cut Them Out of Your Life!* moves its readers through the topsy-turvy world of breast cancer from diagnosis to remission and beyond. Her use of humor and inspirational anecdotes keeps the pages turning.

Lisa is the mother of two boys and resides in Illinois. She is best known for her love of dad jokes and puns, delighting in the mixture of smiles and groans they evoke. Outside of providing support to others navigating their way through breast cancer, Lisa can be found catering to the every whim of a small, but demanding chihuahua.

Connect with Lisa at

https://www.facebook.com/whengoodboobsgobadlisasodyssey.

CHAPTER 8

Describe Your Journey of Being Impacted by Cancer

Pam Carter

"We had been here before!" I thought. About ten years before, the doctor had confirmed what we suspected. "You have very early-stage prostate cancer," he said. After praying and discussing, we decided to have surgery to remove his prostate. That surgery was successful, and the margins were clear. As a result, no follow-up treatments were necessary.

Here we were again. After our yearly physical, the doctor had mentioned that we were both overdue for another colonoscopy. Ron mentioned to her that he was having a little extra gas after eating and she suggested that he have an endoscopy first. We were waiting in recovery after that procedure, and I was getting impatient. This seemed to be taking an awfully long time. When I asked the nurse how much longer they needed to keep Ron, she replied that we could leave soon, but that the doctor would like to have a chat before we left. That chat began with the news that Ron had esophageal cancer. Was he sure? The biopsy would confirm, but he was certain about what he had found. Ron's reaction was, "Well, this is no surprise to God." It was a phrase he used often in the lives of our family.

That began a season of research. Ron was great at that. He did all of our research, for cars, appliances, and TVs, etc.. I have since appreciated the hours he spent doing that and so many other things. We started with an oncologist in Las Vegas, Nevada. That is where we live. After retiring from fifty years as a Pastor, Ron went to work part-time for Pioneer Bible Translators. He loved his job and had great passion for the mission of PBT. Plus, we loved the freedom of retirement to travel internationally and spend time with family and friends. In fact, we had relocated from our last ministry in Northwest Arkansas to Las Vegas to be close to our daughter and her family.

For his seventy-fifth birthday, Ron asked God for ten more years. There is no one I have ever met that loved life more than my Ron. He had so many dreams yet to live, so he found a great surgeon that would take his case at MD Anderson Cancer Hospital in Houston. The surgeon at MDA and the local oncologist worked together to develop Ron's course of treatment, which was to include chemo, radiation and finally, surgery to remove his esophagus. We had a plan and were anxious to get started and be done. As with his previous cancer, we had full confidence that this was a slight detour in our lives, which would soon be back to normal. What a great answer to our prayer; we had the best oncologist in Las Vegas and the department head of gastro surgery at MD Anderson. We were grateful for these brilliant men and that they were a part of our team to restore Ron for our many adventures ahead.

His first chemo appointment was the third week of November 2019. Our fall plans included a trip across the national parks of Utah and a trip to Israel. Plus, we had already reserved vacations in Hawaii and

Spain for spring 2020. When we suggested that we would like to keep all these plans, Dr. Braiteh just gave us a *are you kidding me look*. Little did we know that Covid was just around the corner and our 2020 plans were going to change due to more than Cancer.

We did get to go on our Utah trip in October with our longtime friends. We shared our news, and their encouragement, love and prayers were just what we needed. Once the word spread, we began receiving notes, letters, calls and prayer promises from people around the world. As soon as our church found out, they asked if we would like to be anointed with oil and yes, we did.

Are any of you sick? You should call for the elders of the church to come and pray over you, anointing you with oil in the name of the Lord. James 5:14

We had great confidence that the Lord would heal Ron completely from this disease, just like he had done with prostate cancer.

Ron demonstrated strength and courage during this season. He endured heavy chemo treatments and radiation like a very brave soldier. There were side effects like fatigue, losing his hair and some nausea, but he bore all that very well. We continued to live our lives until March. That is when all our lives changed. COVID!!! ZOOM became a common word in our vocabulary. Ron's Pioneer team from across the USA began to pray through Psalm 91 every day at 4:00 PM via Zoom. *This I declare about the Lord, He alone is my refuge, my place of safety; He is my God and I trust him.* We did and we do trust Him!

I assumed I would go and hang out with Ron at his five-hour chemo treatments, but after the first time, he didn't want me to accompany him.

Ron was a people-person, and he wanted the freedom to talk to other nurses and patients. He would have his chemo on Thursday mornings and come home with a chemo pump. On Friday, we would go back to have his pump removed. Before long many of the staff and patients would greet Ron by name. As he did everywhere we ever went, he made friends and encouraged them. He loved to learn everyone's story. Many times these new friends would join us to hang out, as we sat in the waiting room for our doctor's appointments.

Ron's treatments finished in May 2020. What an awesome day it was! We celebrated! He was CANCER FREE!

The next step was surgery to remove the esophagus, so we flew to Houston for our consultation. Of course, because of the Big C that was affecting everyone, I couldn't go with him for his tests. But they also serve, who only stand and wait. Now, what do you do for a week in a hotel during Covid? We took walks in all the nearby parks and had food delivered to our hotel room in a bag. We enjoyed this restful time together. In the end, they still recommended surgery. Ron wanted to take a break for the summer.

In August, our oncologist scheduled Ron for an endoscopy and a pet scan. Things looked okay, but the treatments had left a lot of damage at the junction of the stomach and the esophagus and there was bleeding. They fixed it and then, they fixed it again. Then, it became unfixable.

One September morning as we were watching Church on TV, Ron was very light-headed and weak. Of course, he wanted to wait until our church service was over, but I insisted we head to the emergency room. He was admitted to the hospital with internal bleeding and his blood level was dangerously low. After transfusions, our doctor directed us to get to Houston ASAP. He was pretty sure the cancer was back.

My daughter accompanied us on the plane ride down and my son flew to Las Vegas and drove our car to Houston. The plan was to get Ron stable and have the surgery. On September 28, the surgeon removed all of Ron's stomach and part of his esophagus. As I look back over the calendar for September 2020, to the end of the year, I find that almost every day was filled with surgery, feeding tube, tests, labs and more tests and labs. Our year was ending, as it had begun.

If I can summarize these months of our lives, I would say how thankful I was for cell phones, nurses, my family, the body of Christ thru His church and for the peace the Lord gave us. That day, when Ron went to the hospital for his consultation, turned into the beginning of his hospital stay. BOOM! I didn't see him again for two weeks. Covid restrictions required that all of our conversations be via cell phone. Ron and the nurses were wonderful in giving me updates all through every day. On the day of his surgery, Ron (remember he wants to know everyone's story) was asking his anesthesiologist how she decided to choose that field. She told him her whole life story; I'm sure prodded by his never-ending questions. She is the first African American head of Anesthesiology at MDA. She was a Christian and they shared their mutual love and trust in Jesus Christ. Before she administered his sedation, she laid her hands on Ron's head and prayed over him. Ron called these divine appointments, and our days were filled with them.

My daughter had done a bunch of research on housing for me during this time. She found two churches in downtown Houston that had ministries to the patients and families of the huge medical complex. Both ministries leased and provided apartments for patients and their families to use. We ended up staying in apartments from St. John's Lutheran and First Baptist over the next many months. I cannot say enough for this amazing ministry to the sick.

DESCRIBE YOUR JOURNEY OF BEING IMPACTED BY CANCER

I was sick, and you cared for me. Matthew 25:39

It was home away from home. These great apartments were fully stocked with all the equipment that a recovering person could possibly need. They checked on us, brought us flowers, cards and offered counselors. All through Ron's surgery, recovery and future stays, these new friends became a part of our story.

The day of Ron's surgery I was alone, but not really. I don't think I ever got off the phone. I received call after call to check in on me. I sat on our balcony overlooking the pool and connected with so many friends and family. The nurses kept updating me on the progress throughout the day. Then, I got the call from Dr. Hofstetter letting me know in detail about the surgery. They found that the stomach contained lesions of cancer, so, instead of removing the esophagus they removed his stomach and part of his esophagus. Finally, that evening I was able to talk to Ron. It was wonderful to hear his voice.

Just five days later, much earlier than expected, they notified me that Ron was being dismissed. I would be feeding him all his food and medicine through a feeding tube, and they would be teaching me how to do all that with Zoom training. Can you say PANIC!!! I have zero skills as a nurse. So, that afternoon I watched as a very nice nurse showed me how to administer everything to a mannequin. "A piece of cake," she said. Fortunately, and I say that ironically (for I know God had it planned), that afternoon, my brother and sister-in-law flew in for a three-day stay.

Together, we picked up Ron, his liquid food, three boxes of supplies, multiple medications and a book of instructions (THINK PHONE BOOK). On my own, I would have been lost and in a complete state of despair. It was overwhelming. Between the three of us and a very patient Ron, we managed.

That first night, we got him into bed with his wedge and pillows and carefully decoded what meds he needed when. Somehow, we managed to make him comfortable. While I cared for Ron, my sister-in-law went through the instructions and wrote out the major steps on a couple of pages while my brother created an excel spreadsheet of what meds were to be given at what time with instructions. It took a village. Even as I write this, I remember the emotion of having this man I loved, in my total care. His well-being depended solely on me. I hadn't felt that kind of responsibility since we brought home our newborns.

Amid this trial and error of caregiving, we managed to laugh. Well, Ron didn't want to laugh….it hurt, but he was amused. My daughter and family came for a couple of days and that cheered us up immeasurably. We did it, although some days it was touch and go; like the time I managed to spray pink medicine all over myself, the bed and Ron. Don't ask! Using a feeding tube takes some practice. This was no easy surgery, and this was the biggest obstacle we faced.

We finally came home. Ron was getting stronger, and we were learning our new normal. We were so grateful for Thanksgiving and Christmas of 2020. By New Year's Day, Ron was off the feeding tube. He was learning how to eat for life. We enjoyed walks, TV sports with no fans, church online and visits from family. We had made it, or so we thought.

In March 2021, we returned to MDA for his six-month follow-up. Dr Hofstetter was amazed by his recovery. Ron had gained weight and energy! Dr. H said he wanted to give Ron every chance to stay healthy, so he ordered DNA testing to determine if Ron carried cancer markings in his DNA. Those results were positive. This brought us back to Houston in April, to make decisions about further treatment. A brand-new immunotherapy had been approved and the doctor thought that this would improve Ron's odds of remaining cancer free. During this April stay, FBC's Hope House just happened to have an open apartment. As always, the Lord continued to go before us and meet our needs.

This new development overshadowed our hearts. We were not done yet. I had so hoped this chapter was finished. It was not to be. Now, fast forward to a few weeks. Ron began to have difficulty swallowing. It quickly accelerated. He lost ten pounds and we returned to Houston for an endoscopy to stretch out the scar tissue that had developed around the surgery site and replace the feeding tube. They also found that the cancer had returned aggressively. It was upgraded to Stage 4. That evening, as I sat in my Hope House apartment, a very tired Dr. Hofstetter called. It was the call no one wants to get, and no doctor wants to make. He was hopeful that this new immunotherapy would give us more time, but Ron wasn't going to get well. That was an awfully long night.

How do you talk about news like this? What is there to say? Mostly, we held hands. We watched a few episodes of THE CHOSEN and sobbed. This was not the ending we wanted, but we truly trusted Jesus with our future. There is a worship song I play that is called, *I'm Blessed*. The words say, "On my best day I'm a child of God and on my worst day I'm a child of God. Oh, every day is a good day. And You're the reason why."

This I declare about the Lord, He alone is my refuge, my place of safety; He is my God and I trust him. Psalm 91:2

Back home, he began undergoing immunotherapy with the goal of slowing the cancer down. This brave man did his best to extend his time with us. Every day we placed it all in the Lord's hands. His timing through this season had been impeccable. His kindness has been overwhelming and His presence was with us every day.

On June 14, Ron woke me up very early. He couldn't sit up. I tried to help him but was just not strong enough. I called the kids, and they came immediately, followed by the ambulance. The hospital found an internal infection around the feeding tube. Antibiotics were administered, his feeding tube was repaired, and he felt so much better.

Our kids and grandchildren were gathering to celebrate Father's Day with us, but we didn't make it. Two days later, Ron's esophagus collapsed leaving him unable to breathe. My best friend, my lover and husband for fifty-three years, saw his Jesus and it took his breath away.

His last night on earth, he was surrounded by his kids and grandkids. The hospital was awesome. They let us all crowd around his ICU bed. Even though he was sedated and on a breathing tube, I know he listened as we held his hands, stroked his forehead and told Grampa stories. There was a lot of laughter among the many tears. Being with his family was his favorite place on earth. But Ron Carter loved the Lord with all his heart, and he was anxious to get on his way to being rid of his cancer.

How is the Carter clan?

II Corinthians 4:16-18 That is why we never give up. Though our bodies are dying, our spirits are being renewed every day. For our present troubles are small and won't last very long. Yet they produce for us a glory that vastly outweighs them and will last forever. So, we don't look at the troubles we can see now; rather we fix our gaze on things that cannot be seen. For the things now seen will soon be gone, but the things we cannot see will last forever.

We will always miss him, although, when we are together, we feel his lingering presence. Francis Weller said, *"We are remade in times of grief, broken apart and reassembled."* We are still in that process. I treasure our fifty-three years together. They weren't perfect and I have some regrets, but in our marriage, we made each other better. I trust, as we trusted, that God still has a purpose and a plan for my life, and He promises to walk through every day with me. There are adventures still ahead.

Cancer is so limited. It cannot cripple love. It cannot destroy peace. It cannot kill friendship. It cannot suppress memories. It cannot silence courage. It cannot invade the soul. It cannot steal eternal life. It cannot conquer the spirit!
Author unknown

Pam Carter

Pam Carter was born and raised in Kokomo IN, the oldest of three surviving children in the Storms home, where faith and service were among some of the most important family values. Pam attended Ozark Christian College where she met Ron Carter. Married in 1968, the young couple set out on a life of service in full-time ministry. For almost thirty years, that ministry career took them from the Midwest to California and back to the Midwest, finally settling in Las Vegas. She is devoted to their two children, and five grandchildren that came along the way.

Pam served in so many critical roles of service as so many ministry spouses do. She has led ministries and service groups within all the churches they were called to serve, spending fifty years leading volunteers to accomplish important achievements. Pam has traveled both nationally and internationally serving in relief roles in places like New Orleans post Katrina, Cambodia, and many other difficult places. Pam has also spoken extensively to both large and small groups around the country.

More than anything though, Pam is about family. She lost the love of her life in 2021.

Connect with Pam at napacpr@aol.com.

CHAPTER 9

Embracing the Impact of Cancer

Patti Schnoor

Hello, I have 3,000 words. This sounds like a lot of words, but I already just used several to let you know that's all I have to tell you about something that was a complete, life-altering event for me, an event that changed my life forever for the better. What?! I just saw you check the title of the book. Cancer?!

Cancer is a bunch of abnormal cells taking over someone's body. It's evasive. Nobody wants that! There can't be anything good about it. Well, for me and my story, a bunch of ugly cells, a surgery, and many months of recovery, although completely unpredictable and hideously scary, has definitely altered my body a bit. More so, it has altered my life. When all was said and done there was the what happened part and then there was the story I could put to the what happened part. What happened was I had cancer. I recovered and I will continue to be screened for cancer. The story I put to it well, that's up to me.

The story begins with me reaching this thing people call middle age and the world as I knew it began to shift dramatically. I had a homebound mom 150 miles away and a dad diagnosed with dementia. I had a husband also suffering from a long-term illness and struggling terribly with depression. Then from nowhere, he suffered a life-threatening lung infection. Everyone was incapacitated, everyone close to me, everyone I loved the most. All I could do is what I had always done when faced with adversity and challenges, I sucked it up, championed on, and stayed in motion. As long as I kept all the plates in the air and spinning, everything would be okay. I just had to keep moving and never dwell on the turmoil. The moments I gave myself time to think about the agony of reality, were always too much to bear. In those moments, the only thing I could do was cry out to God for mercy and ask Him, "Why God? Why? It's too much!"

I asked the question enough, I guess, so that finally my loving Father in Heaven finally gave me the answer. It was a Friday morning before Easter. I was at my mom and dad's house, busying myself with decluttering tables of prayer books that my mom had everywhere. A small, handwritten note bearing my mother's lovely penmanship drifted to the floor from a small rosary book. I picked it up and read it.

"When blows in life chisel away, pray Oh Lord, CHISEL AWAY! And make me Your masterpiece." God's voice came clamoring through in those words, and I fell to my knees sobbing. I am being chiseled, and the chiseling is all about Him forming me into His masterpiece. It's not punishment. It's not punitive. It's transformative. I am God's masterpiece! He is refining me. With that wisdom, I wiped the tears, I stood up, and championed on.

Easter Sunday morning, my husband called, and his voice was full of joy and peace. He felt well enough to go to church and was full of affinity and love for God and for me. My heart tinged with sadness for not being there at that moment. He sensed it and said, "Patti, you are where you are supposed to be. I love you, and you have done everything. You are a saint." He was tired and needed some rest. He laid down on the couch for a nap and went to sleep. While he slept, Jesus took him peacefully home. Upon hearing he passed, I fell to my knees sobbing. I felt the blow of the chisel. That one really hurt. The next big blow came the following year. In December, my mom had a massive stroke and five days later she was gone, too. Blows in life were definitely chiseling away at my very being, and with the heavy grief, my tears persisted, leaving me constantly wondering how I would ever resume my life. How do I pick up the pieces?

Then it was as if an epiphany dawned. Chance! In a stable near to my house, I had a most beautiful and loving paint show horse named Chance. I seldom saw him because I had been so busy, but now it dawned on me that he was what I needed to get back in the saddle of life. I called his trainer and was so happy to be riding him again. To be outside on that absolutely extraordinary Illinois Fall day was the therapy I needed. We were practicing Western Pleasure horsemanship which really just means we were perfecting riding around in circles at different speeds. Chance's trainer was coaching me. Everything felt good and smooth. All was well until he stumbled ever so slightly. I twisted in the saddle and the oddest sensation tingled along my side. I stopped. "What just happened?" The trainer said, "He stumbled a little, but I think he's okay." We finished the lesson. When I dismounted, I had a dull ache across my back and side.

A month later, the pain persisted and while visiting my dad, I awoke nauseated, dizzy, and weak. I was afraid something was really wrong. I decided to try to just make it home to my doctor. I got a little way down the road and then turned around and checked into the ER. They took a scan of my abdomen suspecting kidney stones. As I lay there,

I was fighting back tears not only for physical pain but the emotional pain. I hated being alone in that room. No husband to console me, no mom to hold my hand, and no dad to tell me everything will be O.K. I was alone. Time passed and the doctor emerged. He sat down beside me, and he said, "Well, it's not kidney stones. You have a mass on your right kidney. And it's a big one! You need to get back home and get to a specialist as soon as possible." What took place next was a series of office visits and scans with dye. Then, another office visit where I was again sitting alone with a nurse practitioner who kindly read the results of the CT.

I heard, "blah, blah, blah, carcinoma, blah, blah, blah," Then she said, "Well, that isn't so bad!" "Wait, what about that word that sounded like cancer, isn't it cancer?"

"Well, yes, she said, "it is cancer, but if you are going to have cancer, this is the one you want!"

"What?! I don't want any cancer, what are you talking about, the one that I want."

"Well, you don't need chemo or radiation with this one."

"O.K. What will I need?"

She informed me that a kidney specialist would explain my options at the next appointment. I cried the whole way home. I relented in my plight of sad events. One more blow, chiseling on top of chiseling. How can this be happening to me? Why me?

I met with the urologist, and he showed me the image of the Stage II mass on my kidney and gave me my options for surgery. Another urologist's opinion was to get a biopsy and wait. Making this decision was one of the most mentally agonizing experiences of my life. The voice in my head was talking non- stop, saying nothing good. I didn't research it at all. I was too scared. Avoiding, pretending, and keeping really busy were my best coping mechanisms. I consulted a friend who had battled leukemia. I only had a mild case of cancer compared to her. You know, the one that doesn't need chemo and radiation. I decided it just needed to be gone. I chose to have surgery to remove the tumor and part of my kidney. It's called a partial nephrectomy, and it had been scheduled for a few days after my birthday in mid-March. Once I accepted my decision, I championed on. Plenty of people live with one kidney. I will still have one kidney and maybe a third of the other. It would all be fine.

The day of my surgery arrived, and my loving son traveled to care for me. I don't remember much about it really because, in addition to what was going on with me, there happened to be this whole thing going on in the world, called Covid, and it was causing a pandemic. Things were shutting down exponentially everywhere. Many surgeries, except mine, were canceling. I remember checking in for surgery but remember nothing else until post-surgery in my hospital room. There I was getting my wits about me when an administrative gentleman entered looking very serious, saying that he had something important to discuss with me. What I heard was, "Hospital rules have changed due to the pandemic, and no one is allowed to visit. You cannot have anyone in your room, blah, blah, blah." I listened groggily to his words, as my fight or flight mechanism triggered. I hadn't really even taken full assessment of my state of being nor what had actually been done to my body. All I knew at that moment was that I needed to do whatever it took to leave that hospital. He left and a nurse came into the room. I asked her, "What do I have to do to get out of the hospital?" "You are scheduled to be here two days. You need to be stable and can't go until you can walk around the hospital floor," she replied.

"About that walk, can I use that walker over there?" I asked.

"Yes, you can use the walker, but you will need to walk independent of my help," she said. "In the meantime, is there anything I can get you?"

"I'd like a sandwich, please," I requested. When I had eaten and rested a little, I called her back in the room. "What can I get you?" she asked. "The walker. I am going home today," I asserted.

I have a vivid memory of that walk, an out of body experience really. Stepping onto the floor, feeling the pain, every step is an effort, but once I got going, turning back was not an option. As I rounded the last corner, I felt a wave of nausea and weakness come over me. I stopped. I knew I was close but which door was it? I asked her to point at the room so I could get my bearings. I breathed deep and took those last steps with nothing, but true grit. Later that afternoon, I went home. My son had gotten me through the worst of it and I sent him lovingly on his way. He had much to do in his own life. In the immediate days that followed, I started assessing my condition. I realized I didn't have one incision but five. Why five? Why the heck did he have to make an incision by my belly button. That was one of the few things on my body I actually had always liked. I was super tired, too. Way more tired than I thought I would be. I had one more scan and appointment to make sure the cancer was gone. It was at that follow-up visit that the surgeon asked me how I found out about the cancer in the first place. He said, "most people don't know they have this cancer until it is too late." I told him about Chance and the back pain. He said, "the pain had nothing to do with the cancer. That horse saved your life." My heart swelled with gratitude and love for Chance. The doctor recommended I take it very slow and riding would not be allowed for quite a while which actually turned out to not just be the case for me, but for Chance, too. The reason Chance stumbled was a big deal. He had a neurological condition that would require long term care to overcome. We both would need to recover and recuperate and be a lot less busy.

For my routine, it turned out the pandemic allowed for just that. When I returned to work, my office had become my living room. I spent my days on nonstop Zoom calls with two-dimensional people. With nowhere to go, my physical world shrank significantly, which allowed my spiritual world to grow exponentially. Throughout my life, God and the Holy Family were who encouraged me back into action whenever faced with desolation. This time when I turned back it was with Divine intervention, grace, and velocity. I returned to my holy roots and childhood faith. I got my Catholic back in a big way, and that was when the real healing began. Surrendering myself to Jesus, my Lord, my Savior, His love and consolation flowed into my heart. I reflected on the fact I had been chiseled and chiseled, but I was also reminded that it was for a purpose. I am God's masterpiece! All this chiseling and retooling was just part of Him saving and refining me into an even more spectacular masterpiece.

He also brought into my life from a distance a new beloved and fierce prayer warrior. Through our conversations and prayers, I was able to find comfort and healing. My spirit came back, and I was able to champion on. I just wanted the cancer part behind me. I felt guilty talking about it or dwelling on it.

Afterall, I had had the easy cancer. I didn't need chemo nor radiation. How selfish of me to function as if I really had cancer when so many people that really have cancer spend months of their life being seriously impaired by it. What I had was nothing.

A year passed and I got a call to come in for a CT scan. I couldn't believe it was that time already. Other than being queasy and tired now and then, I was okay. I had convinced myself that this little hiccup of a thing called cancer was all in the past. However, when I found myself in the imaging machine, I started crying uncontrollably as it hummed over my body, and the dye was injected into my bloodstream. Last time I had this, bad things happened. Afterwards, I prayed and kept busy. Word came from a radiologist that I was cancer-free. I wept and smiled and forgot about it again.

Another year passed, and I get a call for another scan. I experienced the now familiar fears, but this time they were realized. The results indicated that there was something there again: same kidney, different location. Several months passed with much waiting, additional screenings of other organs, and further tests. I awaited a prognosis. What if the cancer returned? What if it spread?! Finally, I received positive news that the spot in question was a benign cyst and all was clear!

Shortly after the second CT, my dear friend who survived leukemia asked if I would like to be part of a collaborative book called Embracing the Impact of Cancer. My heart leapt at this request. All I had ever wanted to do my whole life was to be an author. A dream I had abandoned after a crappy grade in a composition class in college and a shifting of my major from journalism to business. I had to go for this opportunity to write again!

At first writing was not easy for me and I became conflicted. It forced me to slow down and embrace not only my cancer, but my life. I realized that when faced with the fear of Stage II cancer in my body, I did the same thing I always did. I absorbed and rebounded. Until I started writing about it, embracing it was nowhere in sight. I barely acknowledged it. Moreover, I see that stuffing my feelings and going through life pretending everything is fine was the whole reason I had cancer!

It was in the writing of this chapter and the unstuffing of those feelings I discovered the fact I have embraced willingly and without hesitation many things in my life. Lots of firsts come to mind...my first dog, my first horse, my first love. All easily embraceable firsts. However, when I think about embracing the impact of cancer, I can say it wasn't the same as a new puppy. I reflected that there are all kinds of welcome impacts in life, and many of those I know I took for granted. There are also the not so welcome or not wanted impacts in life. These are the I don't want to embrace or accept impacts.

What I have come to know is that the greater I can embrace the impact of not just the good stuff, but also the bad stuff like cancer, the better off life is. Cancer and the chiseling from it, is part of the masterpiece that is me. I acknowledge that I am a masterpiece and standing in that moment I have a choice, and I choose to embrace all of it, including cancer. I choose to stay present, courageous, confident, and causing my wellness always, not just once a year.

I don't have to reason with this thing called cancer. I have the opportunity to be completely, well, unreasonable. Cancer, although a hideous and obtrusive interruption, gives the person who has it the ability to expand their thinking beyond death. It provides a glimpse into eternity and the life ever after. It is a catalyst to create greatness.

Eye has not seen; ear has not heard what is possible
for those that believe.
~1 Corinthians 2:9

No matter what, God can create goodness from everything, even malignant cells. You just have to choose. It is your will that chooses, not God's.

What I can say for myself is that in choosing to write these 3,000 words, I got to understand cancer is, and cancer will be, and cancer is not a sad story. It may eventually take me out, but not today, not tomorrow, and not for any time I am aware of in the near future. Therefore, I can live each day in fear of that day, or I can just live each day. I can be present and see life unfold from sunrise to sunset in ways that I never understood or saw before. It's about true triumph, joy, happiness, and allowing life to be imperfect and messy and not allowing bad things to keep me from all the good God has in store for me.

I get what God was up to. I get why I had cancer, and this dis-ease. I have emerged from the chiseling with new purpose and inspiration. Once again, my God shows me just how big He can be, and more so, how big He wants me to be. Oh my gosh! Guess what?! I wrote 3,000 words. You read my story. I am an author!

Patti Schnoor

Patti Schnoor is a farm girl from a little town in Illinois. She loves the earth and all the creatures that dwell among it.

Throughout her childhood, she loved to explore nature by hiking and horseback riding. She has been playing the piano since she was four. Growing up, her favorite end to a day was to sit in an apple tree and gaze into the sunset. In those moments as throughout her life she has felt a definite connection to a Divine Heavenly Power and has never ceased to be amazed by the awe and wonder of the world and what God can do and will do for those who believe.

Patti is dedicated to offering the people she meets the gift of life, love, and spiritual inspiration. Patti has a B.S. in Accounting and Business and an M.B.A. Patti's vocation is to design, develop, and transforms workforce technology systems for the state of Illinois that allow those with life barriers to flourish. She has created new systems which have received Federal recognition and even got her an invite to the White House to talk about transformation. There's no "off switch" for her when it comes to seeing possibilities everywhere. In her down time, Patti still loves to dig in the dirt, play a Beethoven sonata, watch sunsets, and ride her horse, Chance.

Connect with Patti at pschnoorster@gmail.com.

CHAPTER 10

Choosing Unreasonable Hope

Rebecca S. McPherson

For a season, I lived inside my own page-turning novel. Even today it boggles my mind. Every move was fraught with consequences. Two governments were involved. A child was involved. Oncologists, social workers, an army of family and friends marshalled themselves for our case and our cause. Thousands of prayers, a beseeching chorus, bombarded heaven because a life and a future hung in the balance.

Curiously, that life was not my own, though I was the one with cancer.

*** PRE-DIAGNOSIS ***

In 2016, the McPhersons were a family of five, humming along, with three thriving teen and young-adult daughters. Our older two girls, Sydney and Catriona, are homegrown. Our youngest, Nataliya, arrived in our family from Ukraine via adoption many years prior. For our story to make sense, it's useful to know that we hold orphan care and adoption advocacy tenderly in our hearts. Living it out with our hands and feet is like a heartbeat in our household.

Through a confluence of connections to an orphan hosting program, we were invited to serve as a short-term, summer host family for an eleven-year-old boy from a central Asian nation. Our answer was easy: "Yes, of course, we'll host him." Our role was simply to be a happy, safe waystation for this boy for ten days in the summer of 2016.

We fell in love with that dear boy in just that many days. After we said our goodbyes, I turned to my husband and said, "Our family is better with him than without him. We've got to try, don't you think?" Preliminary information suggested he was not available for adoption. If we expressed an interest in adopting him, we asked, could his status be changed? "Maybe" was the reply. Because it is costly, complex, and older children – especially boys – are rarely adopted, orphanages simply do not take the time to make children paper-ready, foreclosing opportunities for hope and a stable future.

Over the next year, we hosted Artur two more times, working diligently on mountains of adoption paperwork. Two years into our intense, longing journey, we progressed just enough to be officially approved for adoption in his home country.

*** DIAGNOSIS ***

I was tired from the relentless paper chase. The days darkened into the early winter of 2019, and I coughed and had a backache. Wheezing and obstructed breathing dogged me as I slept on my right side. The backache I explained away by the cold weather, the shoveling, the carrying more plumpness than is good for my frame. An antibiotic ought to help my cough, I figured, so I scheduled an appointment with the first available doctor. She was attentive and asked thoughtful questions. She said something about covering all the bases and sending me for a CT scan just to rule out anything untoward.

Untoward, as it turns out, was an understatement.

Within a week, the axis of our existence shifted, and we plummeted headlong into a nasty diagnosis. The CT scan showed an ominous-sounding "something," and an MRI visualized even more of that something. A biopsy confirmed mutant lung cells had taken up residence in my liver, ultimately confirming Stage 4 EGFR+ lung cancer. It had invaded lots of my parts: lungs, lymph nodes, liver, spine, and a few other bones, plus my brain.

We gathered our girls, in person and by phone, and I and Tom delivered the dumbfounding news. We cried. We laughed. We sat silently with our tissues. At the center of the storm, I was mindful that everyone would cue off of my tone and demeanor. I encouraged our girls, who were all nearing graduation from one stage of their educations to the next, to be hopeful and to keep their chins up, pointed towards a bright collective future. I ached for the unintended shrapnel wounds I knew this created in everyone.

Intuitively, I knew that communication would be a lifeline for me. I'm also pragmatic. One-off communications with people would not be sustainable, so I shared updates with family and friends via a blogging platform. That simple choice was the single best step I took for my well-being. Having that little platform turned into a nightly place of grace and catharsis as I set out to intentionally find God inside our devastation. His ways, I noted, were as many and varied as the days and the moments they contained. The force of lovingkindness from others was only explainable as a direct pour out from the hand of God.

Social media benefitted me as well. Within days of diagnosis, I was connected via a college classmate to the head of thoracic oncology at one of the most highly-regarded cancer centers in the world. A man of brilliance and compassion, this doctor took time out of his weekend family schedule to call and offer to take me on as a patient.

Within weeks, Tom and I flew to New York City for my first consult. The night before that first appointment, I sobbed like I would never quit, knowing we were marching headlong into uncharted territory. Genetic test results in hand, my oncologist recommended a targeted therapy, Tagrisso, designed specifically to eradicate cells with the genetic mutation my cancerous lung cells harbor.

It worked, phenomenally. After a few short weeks I had no more pain, I breathed more easily, and I stopped coughing. Side effects were modest and entirely manageable. I had not realized how stealthily cancer crept in until I started to feel better. In short, we were all astounded and overjoyed by my evident progress and with my tolerance of the medication itself. Miraculously, I was able to go about my business, living life, even if that life had the omnipresent shadow of cancer lurking.

For me, it felt important to share my perspective – my stance, really – on a few of the deep questions that arise when facing an existential threat like Stage 4 cancer. One statement I made was around my identity, not so much who I am but *whose* I am. I declared that I am not cancer's, I am God's. A second declaration was around prognosis. I affirmed myself to be unreasonably, unapologetically hopeful. While statistics are educated guesses grounded in history, in the end, my days are numbered by God alone, and He will give me every one of those days. Third, and an outcome of the first two: we would continue our international adoption efforts unless and until we heard a clear "no" from God.

On its face that might seem brash, even potentially cruel to a child. In a journal entry from that time, I wrote this:

> *There are days when I stand back and think, "Am I some big weirdo for not feeling tragically distraught over having cancer? Am I living in some dream world where I'm in a huge quagmire of delusional denial? Am I a lunatic or worse – a monster – for believing that it is not only possible but beautiful and right to bring another child into our family at this time?"*
>
> *I'm well-aware of what science says about my scenario, but I am awakened to God's delight in being an odds-buster. He is power and healing and might. He has personally planted the desire in my heart to bring home a beautiful, wounded boy so we can heal together.*

In the months that followed, I had two metastases radiated in my brain, while the remaining fifteen-plus lesions (all of them smaller than a grain of rice) were treated by my targeted therapy. We informed our adoption agency of my status and kept them in the loop on my progress. Six months post diagnosis, with all scans looking profoundly improved, we were approved for the first of our three trips to our son's homeland. I was medically cleared to travel across twelve time zones to an impoverished nation with scant medical resources, and off we went.

Our contact with Artur – mostly random texts sent on other people's phones – was scant over the two years that had passed. He was not aware we were arriving that day in late June, though he had caught wind that it might be soon. His hug and non-stop grin confirmed he was still the same kid – affable, funny, eager for hugs and stories of America, his sisters and dog. Our time together was glorious. Along with another family who, incredibly, were there to adopt our son's best friend at the same time, we brought huge quantities of food to the orphanage every day, enough for the eighty kids who were there that summer. We stayed for hours each day, playing games with the kids, working on crafts, doling out hugs to all who wanted them, playing doctor mom and coach dad to kids who needed some TLC and some semi-organized soccer and basketball skill-building.

Once our requisite ten days of visits were complete, our son wrote a timeline in Russian in the dust settled on the van window, outlining when he thought we might return for our court visit. We jointly speculated October 2019. We were wrong.

*** COLLISION ***

Our facilitator warned us many months earlier that adopting children out of this nation was "a battle against evil." I do not sling words like *evil* around lightly or casually. She was right.

Shortly after arriving home, we were mired in dizzying adoption drama, precipitated by my diagnosis. We had anticipated a head-on collision between adoption and cancer, and now it was upon us. Because our process had already drug on so long, paperwork needed renewal. Our home study agency, responsible for updating the document that is approved by the U.S. government to clear us for international adoption, was initially encouraging of our adoption efforts despite my cancer diagnosis. After internal machinations with their own leadership and processes, however, the agency turned the tide firmly against re-approving us. Our country-specific adoption agency was brought into the discussion, grilled for who knew what when about my diagnosis.

My doctors at home and in New York were asked for copious records and carefully worded statements about my health and their judgment of my ability to parent despite my diagnosis. I will always be grateful that my hero doctor declared: "She is doing well on a once-daily oral therapy for her cancer. I do not consider her cancer to be a contraindication to adoption." Our kids were interviewed. Friends were interviewed. I built a nifty little survey tool (something straight out of my professional wheelhouse) to identify and spotlight folks within our beautiful tribe of supporters who committed to support us in specific ways.

The heart of the issue was always what is in the best interest of this boy. Would he be better off aging out of the orphanage in less than eighteen month's time, turned out onto the streets and permanently unadoptable? Or would he be better off in a stable family with love and resources, even with the possibility of being re-traumatized if his mom died sooner than anyone would like?

We tapped into one of our U.S. Senators for support and advocacy. We worked with a trauma therapist to develop a plan of action for after he was home. We lobbied USCIS and scrambled for assurances after the U.S. government blackballed immigration from our son's country. Our country-specific adoption agency was abruptly closed, due to problems with an adoption program in a different country, forcing us to scramble to find another agency.

Our court date, scheduled for October 2019, came and went as we were mired in chaos. In those months, I had a focal seizure affecting my speech and word-finding abilities, as post-radiation swelling mushroomed in my frontal lobe. It resulted in three-plus months of steroids to reduce the swelling. It took every morsel of every ounce of energy, tenacity and faith we could muster. The sleep disruption of steroids, oddly enough, were a keen advantage just then as I put in feverish hours writing, calling, documenting, advocating, and praying. All the while, our adoption efforts were hanging by a tattered thread.

The prayer was never far from my lips that God would give our family favor to change the life of a boy.

We found that favor through our new adoption agency, hired by us a few weeks after our first agency closed. Fully informed of every detail of our case, they were undaunted in their support of us and our efforts. In late January 2020, a new in-country court date was scheduled. Again, my doctors prepped me with meds and cheered me on my way halfway around the world. Sunday, the day before court, dawned chilly and damp. We worshiped at a local church with our facilitator and son before traveling to an amazing, traditional restaurant.

Hours later, I was in trouble… violently, repeatedly ill. Our wonderful, tenacious facilitator leaned in close to me and whispered, "Is this cancer?" I assured her that it was not, that it was probably just a nasty stomach bug. Paramedics attended to me in my hotel room, but could not start an IV. I heard them translate "central line" to my husband. Tom and I made eye contact that we both knew meant, "Not. A. Chance." Instead, it was agreed that an ambulance would be called, and I would spend the night in the hospital for rehydration, testing and IV antibiotics. The hospital was a squalid place. My IV needle was the stainless-steel, reusable variety. How, I wondered, would anyone with cancer ever survive in such a place?

Hospitalization squashed the possibility of keeping our court date. I was too sick to worry, and our facilitator advocated successfully for the judge to reschedule us to the next day, a Tuesday at the end of January 2020.

One of my journal entries from around that time focused on the notion of submission.

> *Sometimes Submission is an overshadowing of God that brings one to a place of such abject poverty and*

circumstantial misery that Submission is no longer a choice... it is a place. This place called Submission was well beyond the reach of normal emotions like stress or fear or mortifying embarrassment. It was even beyond emotional choices like hope and grit. It was a floaty kind of place, and I was untethered from the usual lens through which I peer at the world. The rapid-fire Russian swirling around me held no meaning. The sea of faces coming in and out above me meant nothing to me, save for Tom, Artur, and our beautiful facilitator. I think I said, "I'm sorry" a lot, until sorry wasn't even close to enough.

The place called Submission has a river running through it. Its name is Peace. That floatiness, that lack of mooring to anything familiar made way for the Peace that surpasses understanding to come rushing in. Submission, with all of its outward disgustingness, is a place of beauty to be entered into meekly and bare-souled. I did not leave it unchanged. I do not want to go back there, but I will if I must because there is Peace there.

By God's grace, I rallied enough to make it through court. The judge quickly moved to approve our petition to adopt our son. Not a single health question was asked.

After traveling back to America, my husband returned six weeks later to bring our son home, nearly four years after we first met him. It was March 2020, and the COVID-19 pandemic was marching its way around the world. My doctors deemed it unwise for me to travel. My rock-solid husband traveled one last time across oceans and continents. Enroute, we learned that he'd be quarantined the entire time in country, save for a special exemption to attend the exit interview at the U.S. Embassy. U.S. government approval came just in time, including a special exemption for adoption immigration for our son's blacklisted nation.

In one final stroke of God's favor upon this adoption, my husband and our new son flew out on the final flight from the country before COVID-19 closed the borders to air travel.

*** THREE YEARS LATER ***

Artur has been home three years now. He is thriving, as am I.

My son once asked me if I would ever sacrifice him. He was studying the Bible story of Abraham and Isaac, which focuses on questions of trust and sacrifice. I paused and considered carefully before I answered. God, I said, already tested me around the question of whether I would sacrifice my son. God had laid a promise on my heart that he would make Artur our son. I said that God tested my trust in Him through cancer. Because it was so clear to me that he would be our son, God gave me a choice. Would I doubt God and not bring Artur home because cancer is big, bad and scary? I told Artur we made a decision to trust God that, somehow, He would make it work out, even though we didn't know how.

I didn't say the rest of this to Artur because it was beyond my ability to explain in the simple English he needed. We had such clarity around adopting this boy that I imagined I knew exactly how God would make it happen. I foolishly thought the Lord was testing us by making Artur and our family wait and doggedly persevere. I thought I knew all sorts of things because I was all gumption-y and assumption-y. The trouble is, I didn't really listen to God after His promise landed in my heart. Because I didn't listen, I couldn't fully walk by faith.

Then I got cancer. I started listening for God's real question. It was simply worded: *Will you put your faith and trust in me that I will keep my promise?*

God's corollary questions were something like this: Will you lay your Artur, your son whom you love, down, and will you trust me and not yourself? Will you do all I ask, knowing that every flashing-red indicator points to a brutal sacrifice of the boy whom you love? Will you do all I ask, knowing that in the natural world Stage 4 lung cancer is a checkmate on adoption? Will you risk the apparent worldly prospect of having to leave him there forever, breaking all kinds of hearts in the process, because you trust in me? Will you risk a future that you may not be there to witness because I promised Artur not just a mother, Beca, but an entire family and community who will love and care for him?

Beca, will you put your faith and trust in me? I will do these things. Because, my beloved child, I am a covenant maker and a promise keeper.

Beca Solberg McPherson

Beca Solberg McPherson is many things to many people: devoted wife, proud mom of four, orphan advocate, loyal friend, freelance strategy wonk, and cancer thriver. Above all, Beca is a child of God. She delights in sharing her story of the collision of cancer and her family's international adoption efforts. Since her lung cancer diagnosis in 2019, she's used her story as a platform to tell of God's goodness and faithfulness. She is a frequent speaker and teacher at her church, using her family's beautifully unique story as a launching pad for people to discuss their own lives' collisions. A seasoned facilitator of complex discussions that have elemental roots, Beca's gift is helping people grapple with deep questions of lived-out faith, encouraging others to trust that their faith has every reason to be unreasonably hopeful.

Beca is a 1990 graduate of Dartmouth College, where she majored in Sociology. She went on to graduate from the University of Chicago Booth School of Business in 1995, with concentrations in Business Policy and Marketing. For 25 years, she has partnered with clients to support them in their strategic planning objectives. Fun fact: Beca was "remote" before remote employees were even a thing. Her long-standing practice is to manage her client engagements primarily from her home office, enabling her to [most days, anyway] keep a healthy balance in her many-things-to-many-people reality.

Beca is grateful for enduring relationships in every dimension of her life. She always welcomes more. Connect with Beca on Facebook: https://www.facebook.com/beca.mcpherson.

CHAPTER 11

Tools for the Fight

Ronn Hollis

Let's begin with the end in mind, shall we? Cancer sucks, it's not easy for you or your family, BUT you learn a lot about yourself, and it's possible for you to beat it!

With that out of the way, my name is Ronn and I was diagnosed with Stage 4 Adenocarcinoma of the Lung in August of 2014. My path to survivorship included a year and a half of chemotherapy, two rounds of radiation, and immunotherapy as a chaser. As I write to you today, I have just completed my latest six-month CT scan where the oncology team emphatically reports *No Evidence of Disease!* That's where I am now. Getting here wasn't easy, but I was given a few mental tools from other survivors during my journey and I want to share them and a few of my own with you to be helpful.

No one expects to hear the words you have cancer. In my case, the doctors found it by accident as they were doing an ultrasound to check my gallbladder. Something unusual showed up on the scan, and the technologist casually excused herself, said "I'll be right back, Mr. Hollis." She went to get the doctor and, before I knew it, I was in the emergency room about to have almost two liters of fluid removed from my chest. Only after a series of tests on that fluid would I have my diagnosis. I spent the next eight days in the hospital before I could go home and start my cancer fight.

When I met my oncologist, Dr. David Spigel, he talked about the Stage and location of my tumors. I learned they were inoperable and that, for now, radiation was not an option. "We are going to try chemo" is what I remember him saying. Upon hearing it presented THAT way, I remember my inner dialogue rambling on with something like "TRY?! What do you mean TRY?!" Let's just say I was ready for a fight. "I have a wife, four amazing young children, and I'm forty-seven. We're gonna do more than try!" I didn't really know it then, but I'm now convinced that attitude is everything when fighting cancer, so that's where we are going to spend our time together. The doctors and nurses are on your side, you do your part to keep your mind clear and in fighting mode. Don't go down too many rabbit holes of pity, and *what ifs* as that isn't helpful. Instead, let's focus on your new reality ~ what lies ahead in the coming months ~ and let me give you a few of those tools I talked about.

First, please know that EVERYTHING changes when you are told you have cancer. Your priorities change, your outlook changes, your job, how you handle your time, your wish list and, most importantly, your relationships change … and that's where our tools begin.

Frank's Rule:

Frank was an old friend who, coincidentally, beat cancer back in the '80s when few people did. I would describe him as a big-hearted, pragmatic, methodical, retired Navy aviator that always made sure he had a plan. No matter what. When I got home from the hospital, Frank was the first to call. "I'm on my way over to pick you up for lunch and I'm twenty-five minutes out," he said. I countered with "Frank, that sounds great, but I'm lying on the couch connected to an oxygen machine so I don't think I can make it." Never one to take NO for an answer, Frank said, "Well, they gave you one of those little O2 tanks on wheels didn't they? It's time to try it out, I'm now twenty minutes out." He won. It was at that lunch, with my little tank and canula in tow, that Frank explained to me that I needed to *find my people*. I was confused then, but now I'll tell you it's some of the sagest advice a friend has ever given me.

If your parents were like mine you were taught not to judge other people so you wouldn't be judged yourself. I'm here to tell you that rule goes out the window when to have cancer. Frank told me not to be surprised if some of my closest friends and family pulled back or even stopped communicating completely once they learned of my diagnosis. "Don't try and figure it out" Frank said. "It could be that a cancer diagnosis is THEIR biggest fear for themselves or they can't comprehend the idea of you with cancer ... they may not want to say the wrong thing so, they choose not to say anything at all. Just know that it will happen, and you need to let it go." Not to dwell on the negative, Frank went on to explain that "there will be friends and family that COMPLETELY DIVE IN to help in SO many actionable ways!"

I want you to know that Frank was right and gave me such a boost that day by giving me that insight. Knowing this ahead of time will keep you from having your feelings hurt and wondering what YOU did to have some friends pull away from you after you got sick. It's not you, it's them. Don't be mad either as you don't have time for that. Within days, I began to see exactly what Frank meant. People pulled away for sure. It hurt a little but, knowing that it wasn't because of something I did, it made it a little easier. More importantly, the inverse also happened. I had friends reach out from all over and even come to our house to ask how they could help. One friend took my wife's car to have the brakes done. The bill? "No charge" said the mechanic who had learned of my story. Another showed up with a new deep freezer from Costco FULL of food. He and another friend unloaded it and plugged it up in our house! Our kids ate like royals for weeks! There are more stories I could tell, but just know that I hope you have more people *lean in* than *lean out* during your cancer fight. Knowing that it would happen was so important for me. I hope it's helpful to you.

Emotions are Good!

Another tip I'd offer is about emotions and how to use them to your benefit. A cancer fight is a marathon and not a sprint. You will have ups and downs along the way, but for me, I learned to even out those lows. Remember the former basketball coach at North Carolina State named Jimmy Valvano? He had been diagnosed with an extremely aggressive cancer. Before he passed, he gave a remarkable speech on television. In that speech, he said something that always stuck with me.

> *To me, there are three things we all should do every day. If you do them every day of your life, you're going to ... What a wonderful ... Number one is laugh. You should laugh every day. Number two is think, you should spend some time in thought. And number three is you should have your emotions moved to tears. Could be happiness or joy, but think about it. If you laugh, you think, and you cry, that's a full day. That's a heck of a day. You do that seven days a week, you're going to have something special.*
> ~ Jimmy Volvano

As I started my own cancer fight, I would often reflect on that and, one day, decided to put that into action. I thought about my mind, heart, and soul and what medicine I could give them. That idea of laughing, thinking, and crying came to mind so I made a goal to do those things twice a day – every day.

How do you do that? Well, for me, YouTube was my friend! I would routinely be moved to tears watching home movies of military personnel coming home to surprise loved ones with their presence. A military mom or dad coming home from a deployment to surprise their young child at school got me every time! I'd also watch funny pet tricks and comedians to get my laughs in. Find some that work for you and give it a try! Be faithful about it, do it every day, and you'll find you are able to manage the highs and the lows more easily.

Here's something I want you to know today: You have more control of your life than you may think. Cancer wants you to think it now controls every aspect of your day, but it doesn't. Yes, it's a life change, BUT you can still grow, still laugh, still cry, and above all, you can and should actively love those around you. Talk to them more and tell them or show them that you love them. You won't regret it, and neither will they.

What's Your Battle Cry?

My guess is that the above question gave you a chuckle. Who has a battle cry?! I suspect you may be saying. Well … YOU should and here's why: During my first few rounds of chemo, I found myself sick and exhausted and I got so TIRED of those feelings. I know this sounds crazy, but I got SO sick and tired of feeling sick and tired, I just decided I was going to get better starting THEN! That feeling morphed into my personal battle cry of RALLY RALLY RALLY! After each round of chemo, when I found myself down for the count and mad about feeling that way, I would literally tell myself it's time to RALLY RALLY RALLY! I declared at that moment that I was going to get better. What started as an idea born out of anger, became an integral part of my journey to getting better.

I still use my battle cry on a daily basis. In fact, a close friend had those words made into a sign that I keep in my office and reflect on daily. It's a small thing, but it's powerful and I want that power to be yours.

You Can Do It!

Cancer has taught me many things and I'm thankful for it. If I had to choose one thing to leave with you it's this: Decide what or who is most important to you, focus on that, and let the little, nagging things in life melt away. I spent too much time pre-cancer trying to solve those meaningless life problems that didn't add value to me or anyone else. That's a waste of time and we don't have time to waste! Be intentional about how you spend your day. Focus on those that support you and be sure to support them too. Be purposeful with your emotions and let them work for you. Laugh and cry … every day. It's good medicine and you will be better for doing it. Love actively. Show those that care about you just how much you care for them too.

Cancer gave me the tools to live intentionally, and you can have that too. It's so much better to think and live that way. You can do it!

Ronn Hollis

Ronn Hollis is an entrepreneur, healthcare executive, and big believer in helping others in their fight against cancer. After being diagnosed with Stage 4 cancer in 2014, he has focused his time and effort on supporting others with tools to help them in their own cancer fight. He is a husband and father and dedicated to being an encouraging helper for others.

Connect with Ronn at https://www.linkedin.com/in/ronn-hollis-mmhc-50856b.

CHAPTER 12

My Lung Cancer Story

Stephen Huff

As I sit down to author my story, I can hardly believe the words that come to mind. *My lung cancer story* - it sounds like a chapter in someone else's life. Yet here I am, at the age of thirty-five, facing a reality that I never thought would happen to me. I was the epitome of health - a former college and professional baseball player, with a passion for taking care of my body through exercise and healthy eating. But on June 1, 2017, my life changed forever when I was diagnosed with stage IV lung cancer.

Looking back, I can see now that my cancer journey started long before my diagnosis. I had been experiencing shortness of breath for a while, but I ignored it, thinking it was just a sign of aging or allergies. I learned to cope with the symptoms, and eventually, I didn't even realize they were there. It wasn't until my fiancé (now wife) Emily noticed a hard lump above my collarbone that I was forced to confront the reality that something was seriously wrong. After months of tests and misdiagnoses, I finally received the devastating news that I had stage IV lung cancer that had already spread to my lymph nodes, liver, and bones.

One of the most difficult things about my diagnosis was the loss of control over my life. Cancer is a disease that can make you feel powerless and uncertain about your future. Just months before my diagnosis, I had a new job, a new home, and plans to marry the love of my life in just a few months. I never could have predicted that I would be facing a life-threatening illness instead. It's a sobering reality that all late-stage lung cancer patients face. There is no cure, and every day is a battle.

Despite the harsh reality of my situation, I never lost hope. I was diagnosed with a specific and rare type of lung cancer driven by a genetic mutation known as the ALK Positive rearrangement. This allowed me to receive a new form of treatment called targeted therapy. Unlike traditional chemotherapy, targeted therapy is an oral tablet with minimal side effects. It has allowed me to live a relatively normal life. I wake up each day, drink too much coffee, kiss my wife and son goodbye and head off to work full-time. Most importantly, I am blessed to be called a husband and a father. Targeted therapy has given me not only the ability to live a normal life, but also a tremendous sense of hope. These miracle drugs have given me precious time with my family and friends, all with an exceptional quality of life. It's why I'm so grateful for the work that researchers and advocates alike do in the field of cancer therapeutics. This desire to find a cure offers hope and excitement to patients like me who are fighting for their lives.

My cancer diagnosis has taught me many valuable lessons. I would never call cancer a gift, but I can say that it has been a blessing in disguise. Since my diagnosis, I have received so much love and support that I can honestly say I appreciate life more than I ever did before. I am a stronger person because of this battle, and it has opened my eyes to the importance of advocacy and the meaning of true love in this world.

I will spend the rest of my life advocating for awareness of my disease. I firmly believe that awareness can have an impact on the lives of others, and I want to do my part to ensure that others don't have to go through what I have. As I tell anyone that asks how I get through this rollercoaster of emotions and fears, I share a quote from Confucius, "We have two lives, and the second begins when we realize we only have one." I implore everyone I meet to reclaim living in the present tense and to enjoy all the beautiful things that life offers.

I can't help but feel grateful for the life that I have been blessed with. It's been over five years since my diagnosis, and I am still here, alive and thriving. I have a beautiful wife, a remarkable son, and a career that I love. There are still struggles, of course, the anxiety of regular scans, the fear of relapse, and the uncertainty of what the future holds. I have learned to live in the present and appreciate every moment I am given.

One of the things that has helped me on this journey is the support of my loved ones. My wife, Emily, has been my rock throughout this entire process, providing endless love, encouragement, and strength when I needed it the most. She has been my partner in this fight, and I am grateful for her every day.

I could not have made it this far without her unwavering love and support, and I am forever grateful for her presence in my life.

When I received my diagnosis of stage IV lung cancer, Emily was there with me every step of the way. She held my hand tightly as we listened to the doctors explain my treatment options, and she never left my side during the many long hours spent in the hospital. She became my rock, my cheerleader, and my caregiver all rolled into one.

I quickly learned that a cancer journey is not just an individual experience, it is a journey that the entire family takes together. Emily took on the role of caregiver with such grace and strength, never once showing any signs of exhaustion or stress. She took care of everything, from scheduling my appointments to making sure I had my medications on time. She would even stay up late researching new treatments and clinical trials for me to consider.

Except her role was not limited to the practical side of things. She also provided emotional support and comfort when I needed it the most. There were times when I felt like giving up, but Emily's words of encouragement and her unwavering belief in me helped me find the strength to keep going. She was always there to lend an ear, to offer a hug, and to remind me that I was loved.

Through all the ups and downs of my cancer journey, Emily has been my constant source of hope and inspiration. She has shown me what true love and devotion look like, and I am in awe of her strength and resilience. I cannot imagine going through this journey without her by my side.

In the end, cancer has brought us even closer together as a couple. We have learned to cherish every moment and to never take each other for granted. I know that I am lucky to have such an incredible wife, and I am grateful for her every day.

To anyone going through a cancer journey, I cannot stress enough the importance of having a supportive partner by your side. Cancer can be a lonely and isolating experience, but having someone to share the journey with can make all the difference. I am forever grateful for my wife Emily, and I know that our love will only continue to grow stronger as we face whatever challenges the future may hold.

I also have an incredible network of family and friends who have been there for me in so many ways. They have helped with meals, childcare, and emotional support, allowing me to focus on my health and my family. Cancer can be isolating, but my family and friends have never let me feel alone in this battle.

Throughout my journey, I have also found solace in connecting with other cancer patients and survivors. We share a bond that only those who have gone through this experience can understand. I have made lifelong friendships with people who understand the struggles and the triumphs of this disease.

My cancer journey has also taught me the importance of self-care. Before my diagnosis, I was always on the go, pushing myself to be the best in everything I did. Cancer forced me to slow down, to prioritize my health and my well-being. I now make time for exercise, meditation, and rest, knowing that taking care of myself is essential to my survival.

As I reflect on my experience with cancer, I am filled with gratitude for the medical advancements that have allowed me to receive targeted therapy. These drugs have given me the ability to live a relatively normal life, and I am hopeful that more targeted therapies will be developed for other forms of cancer. But I am also aware of the disparities in cancer care and the need for increased funding and resources for cancer research. Every patient deserves access to the best possible treatment options, and it is our collective responsibility to advocate for better cancer care.

I don't know what the future holds for me, but I am confident that I will continue to fight with every ounce of strength that I have. Cancer has taught me that life is a precious gift, and I intend to make the most of every moment that I am given.

As I close my story, I want to offer a message of hope to anyone who may be facing a cancer diagnosis. You are not alone. There is an army of doctors, nurses, researchers, and advocates fighting for you. There are also countless other cancer patients and survivors who understand the struggles and can offer support and encouragement. Cancer may be a part of your story, but it does not define you. You are strong, resilient, and capable of facing this challenge head-on. Don't be afraid to ask for help when you need it, and never lose hope. There are new treatments and advancements being made every day, and we are all in this fight together.

Although my journey with cancer has been a rollercoaster ride, I am proud of the progress I've made and the person I've become. I have come to appreciate the little things in life that I once took for granted, like the sound of my son's laughter or the smell of fresh coffee in the morning. I am grateful for every day that I wake up and get to spend with my loved ones, knowing that it's not something that everyone gets to experience.

Being diagnosed with cancer has also given me a newfound appreciation for my community of family and friends. They have become my heroes, they are the ones who have helped me through some of my darkest days. I will never forget the kindness and compassion that they have shown me throughout this journey. They have been my rock, and I am forever grateful for their dedication and commitment to loving and supporting our family.

Throughout my journey, I have also learned the importance of mental health. Cancer not only affects your physical health but also your mental well-being. The diagnosis can be overwhelming, and it's essential to take care of your mental health just as much as your physical health. It's important to find support from family, friends, or a professional therapist who can help you navigate the emotional rollercoaster that comes with cancer.

I have also learned to find joy in the simple things in life. Cancer has a way of putting things into perspective and reminding you of what really matters. I try to make the most of every moment and enjoy the little things that make life special. Whether it's a sunset, a good book, or a hug from my son or wife, As I move forward, I will continue to cherish every day and live my life to the fullest.

Thank you for taking the time to read my story. I hope that it has offered some insight into the journey of a cancer patient and the importance of advocacy and support. Above all, I hope that it has offered a message of hope and resilience to anyone who may be facing a similar battle.

Stephen Huff

Stephen Huff is a remarkable individual. Who had been diagnosed with stage IV lung cancer at the age of twenty-nine. Despite battling metastatic cancer that had spread from his lungs to lymph nodes, liver, and bones, Stephen remained determined and resilient, never losing hope. He has a rare type of lung cancer driven by a genetic mutation known as the ALK Positive rearrangement.

Before his diagnosis, Stephen lived an active and healthy lifestyle, having played college and professional baseball and consistently making healthy choices. His journey with lung cancer began a few years before his diagnosis, as he started experiencing shortness of breath. However, as his symptoms worsened, he eventually sought medical attention, leading to a confirmation of his stage IV lung cancer.

Despite cancer taking away the feeling of control in his life, Stephen continues to fight and find joy every day. As a husband, father, and working full-time, he has been on targeted therapy for over five years, allowing him to live everyday life with minimal side effects.

Stephen considers cancer a blessing in disguise because it has made him appreciate life and advocacy more than ever. He now advocates for cancer awareness and living life to the fullest. Stephen encourages everyone he meets to reclaim living in the present and enjoy all the beautiful things life offers without waiting for something catastrophic to happen. Stephen's story is a testament to the power of hope, resilience, and the importance of living life to the fullest.

Connect with Stephen at http://thehuffproject.org.

CHAPTER 13

My Raison D'Etre After Cancer

Susan Sullivan Danenberger

If I had one wish, it would be for everyone to experience what I have. Not the stage 4 cancer, but the power of love, prayer, and chasing dreams to the fullest. If I hadn't been diagnosed with cancer, I would never have experienced and felt the love, support, and friendship that has been given to me from so many people. I would not have had the driving force to step out of the box and try daring experiences. It seems so simple, yet it took facing death to gain this fresh perspective that has revolutionized my life!

Before I had cancer, I designed this new life that I wanted—to build a winery on my Centennial farm and give it a new legacy. I would go to bed with a vision, and each night in my sleep, I would ferment the grapes and imagine spaces filled with people sharing memories together and drinking my wine. My winery, Danenberger Family Vineyards, was my raison d'etre—or as I liked to call it, my "raisin d'etre" (a play on the traditional French phrase because I am a winemaker). I opened my winery in the fall of 2013 with a quintessentially perfect opening day: glorious weather, new customers who became new friends, a grape delivery of three tons of Traminette, and the local newspaper to cover it all. I had planned to be a hostess, entertaining guests with wine pouring, but instead, I ended up crushing and pressing grapes in my purple off-the-shoulder dress while customers watched. It was unexpected but memorable! And I knew things would only get better!

My winery had been open for less than a year when I found a pea-sized lump in my left breast while taking a shower in the spring of 2014. I can't explain why, but I knew immediately that something wasn't right. Although it didn't show up on a mammogram, a sonogram and biopsy were performed right away. I still remember the nervous chatter from my radiologist as he distracted me with wine topics, but the look on his face gave it away—he already knew it was cancer but couldn't tell me until it came back from pathology. The rest of that day played like a short film in slow motion. I could barely move, so I sat on the steps outside the medical building and called three people (Kim, Debbie, and Jay) whom I knew had survived cancer. They were my shoulder to cry on in those early days when I didn't know what would happen next.

I barely remember the weeks following. My cancer was caught early, was not invasive, and was fueled by estrogen. Easy-peasy! Let's just get that part out and get back to my life, right?! Even my surgeon thought this was going to be simple. When I mentioned a double mastectomy, he thought I was overreacting. He knew I had just began living my dream, and he felt a lumpectomy would be more conducive to this new lifestyle. I will admit, I wasn't ready to slow down for anything, but when the margins did not come back clear, I didn't have a choice.

My doctor recommended thirty rounds of radiation, plus six rounds of boost radiation. It sounded effortless. I would lie in a molded form each morning from June to August, get zapped by invisible forces for a few minutes, and go back to work for the rest of the day. I was wearing rose-colored glasses proudly, so I stepped into this first "real" fight with breast cancer without having cancer advocates, patients, or survivors to help guide me. I didn't do research. I didn't want to be a cancer patient. I wanted to get back to my newly opened winery and the dream I had finally created my life and reason for being. I was determined that a positive outlook would make a difference, so I came up with a self-challenge to make it fun. I called it Rock On Radiation. I would wear a different pair of stilettos to each radiation treatment. I took a picture and posted it on social media with my pink flamingo mascot from my best friends, Juliann and Jennifer.

What I didn't expect to happen was that other people would be just as excited by my game as I was. The technicians and the other women waiting for treatment each morning with me would check to make sure I didn't repeat my heel choice. I looked forward to seeing these same people for twenty minutes each day; they became my clique and my first support system. They realized the severity of what was happening to me during each radiation treatment before I did. I am beholden to those guardian angels on Earth, all breast cancer patients or survivors, who offered tips to get me through the burnt skin and exhaustion phases with little gifts of kindness. I dipped my toes into becoming part of the cancer community and found my first cancer friend, Kim C, who still offers my advice and hugs as she, too, continues to fight cancer.

As it turns out, radiation wasn't the right choice at that time, and accepting this treatment would negatively affect my life from then on. I was all too ready to trust the statistics from my radiation oncologist—the 2% recurrence rate would not apply to me. HA! Take that, Cancer! I have a life to get back to!

The joke was on me, when cancer returned in 2016, right before grape harvest. I put off my mastectomy to finish harvest and fermentation, thinking it wouldn't spread that fast (because my first cancer growth was tiny). By the time I slowed my life down to take it seriously, it had spread. I heard the wake-up call and found a top-rated cancer center two hours away. My double mastectomy surgery on December 9, 2016 was fraught with complications from the radiated skin and lymph node removal. I was truly surprised when they sent me home the next day with paperwork to call after the holidays and schedule the next course.

On Christmas Eve, I went into my local ER, presenting with a fever and a left breast that was beet red and hot to the touch. The doctors knew it was an infection, but no one wanted to step into that quagmire as I was a cancer patient at another center. They offered me the option of an (expensive) ambulance ride to St. Louis or to drive myself. It was a pivotal moment. I truly believe this was the moment I decided I had to do it all myself and stop asking for help. I left feeling alone, terrified, and angry.

I spent the holidays in Barnes hospital, far away from family and friends, with a severe post-op infection and vancomycin IVs. My medical team of doctors and residents were basically hands-off, but I was determined to get better and get the hell out of there. That was the only time I ever felt sorry for myself. From that point on, I was positive and knew I was going to fight this cancer no matter what the statistics or doctors said. I would walk the halls for hours with my IV pole, visiting with anyone who would talk. I made social media posts like everything was great and I was in good spirits. "Fake it until you make it" was my motto.

During those particularly difficult years, when some of my treatments and medications failed, I changed my mindset from trying to get rid of cancer to learning to live with it. I have been metastatic (stage 4) for six years. Cancer will be part of my life for the rest of my life. I'm proud of that. I have had the privilege of participating in several research trials. I always say yes! This research could potentially save lives by providing better medicines and treatments for future patients. I have been through several IV chemos, pulmonary embolisms, hair loss, three different oral anti-cancer medicines (CDK4 & 6 inhibitors), monthly injections of estrogen inhibitors, bone meds, hypercalcemia meds, monthly IV immunoglobulin therapy, lung infections, platelet transfusions, leukopenia, neutropenia, clinical trial rejections, acupuncture, and even eastern/plant medicine to slow down cancer.

My story is not a sob story about what I have been through but is a success story about how I have been through it. I have become more active in the decision-making. I even made choices to stop one of my anti-cancer drugs when the side effects became intolerable. I want to live, but I also want to live well, and I felt that not all my medication was allowing me to do so, therefore I sought out more ways to maintain my quality of life and continue to make wine.

This led me into considering how to fix the botched breasts I was left with during the first reconstruction surgery. I didn't feel like myself. It may sound superficial, but I missed wearing the clothes that made me feel like the woman I was before I had cancer. My first plastic surgeon was afraid the post-op infection would negatively affect his patient statistics. It was obvious he didn't want to have me as a patient. He treated me with aloofness when I went in for my visits. When it came time for implant reconstruction, he slapped them in and stitched me up, with little regard to how they looked. My breasts were left uneven, at different heights and sizes, with deep gouges and dents in both. I had my drains in for more than forty-five days and was left with a permanent crease from them crossing over my nipple on the left breast. This would become deeper and more pronounced (even through my clothes) when I flexed while doing simple tasks like pouring wine for a customer, pruning grapevines, or moving equipment in the winery. I felt very uncomfortable! It wasn't just a question of vanity; part of my sense of identity was my fashion and my stilettos (my nickname is Stilettos In The Vineyard for a reason). My first surgeon didn't care. He just wanted to be finished and told me there was nothing that could be done to fix the problems with the reconstruction. I didn't know my rights. I didn't know I could find another surgeon and asked to have more aesthetically pleasing breasts (for me).

A customer at my winery told me about two female plastic surgeons in my community. I went to both and was thrilled to learn that Dr. Nicole Sommer at SIU plastic surgery had a fellowship in breast reconstruction and honestly thought she could help me look more like myself again! She advised me that it would take several surgeries, using the Ryan Flap procedure, scar removal, and fat grafting. She (and her residents Dr. Amanda Dawson and Dr. Tim Daughtery) are miracle workers! My breasts aren't perfect, but they look fabulous in clothes, and I finally can buy reconstruction bras. Which led me to the next part of my life-with-cancer journey—learning how to thrive!

My next wonderful lesson from cancer: If you're finding it hard to have hope, surround yourself with people you know will lift you up. In 2019, my doctors sponsored me to walk in a New York Fashion Show for bra and loungewear company AnaOno to shed a light on the options of reconstruction and on our very talented surgeons in the community. During this endeavor, I developed deep friendships with my doctor, Nicke Florence, and talented SIU photographer, Maria Ansley. They have become my "ride or die" friends. They understand and support me; even their text messages are a hug from God. They have taught me that you shouldn't be afraid to share how you're truly feeling and you don't always have to be strong. For the first time since being diagnosed with cancer, I learned to share more of my journey with those around me. Because of the love from Maria, Nicke, and Nicole, I experienced walking the runway in New York Fashion Week!

When I walked in NYFW, I met the other models who were also metastatic, and a whole new world opened for me! I met so many different types of women all over the world who understood what I was going through and could give me advice with treatments, bras, and even makeup and skin products. Before that, I didn't feel like most breast cancer survivors because I was still fighting it. Living with cancer is a lot different from living after cancer. My treatments will end when I die. But because of cancer, I met a cancer community of women who are doing great big things in this world! One of them is the AnaOno designer, Dana Donofree, who has since made a very sexy reconstruction bra and named it after me (The Susan). It is very beautiful and lacy, but my favorite thing about the bra is the way the lace on each side by the armpit covers the area where my lymph nodes were removed, so it doesn't show the flabby skin. I have continued to promote boob-inclusive women's products back in my community by having an AnaOno fashion show at my winery so other women would be made aware of these bra options for reconstruction patients.

I have spent the last four-plus years being very active and philanthropic in Central Illinois by advocating and raising funds and awareness for breast cancer research and breast cancer reconstruction options. I have become an active board member of our regional American Cancer Society, raising thousands in my own campaigns each year. I have been working hand in hand with SIU School of Medicine to raise awareness for the rights of patients for reconstruction each October. We have had benefits, events, and fashion shows to bring empowerment to women cancer patients and raise monies for areola tattoos for women who can't afford it.

In December 2022, I passed my six-year mark of living with metastatic breast cancer. I am one of the 22% that have made it this far and am now considered a Long-Term Survivor. The ten-year survival rate drops to 13%. My treatments are aimed at slowing down the cancer's rate of growth as much as possible, without destroying myself in the process. Some of the meds I am now on have come out in the last few years, and I keep hoping there will be more new ones in the future from current research.

From the outside looking in, my professional life has blossomed while surviving these eight years with metastatic breast cancer. My winery has grown into a popular destination with a large music venue and bourbon bar. Each year, I feel pride (and relief) when I release the next vintage of wines—each one always becoming my new favorite. I wake up each morning knowing I am part of something bigger—my wine and the beautiful spaces I created are making people happy and giving them meaningful memories with family and friends. It is more than just my job; it is my purpose and my dream. But cancer led me to discover more purposes and passions in life—by making a difference in this world by acts, great and small. Without cancer, I wouldn't have as strong of a relationship as I do with my mind and body, and I wouldn't have started helping others who are going through cancer treatment or survivorship. Cancer is an experience that never truly leaves you. But I have chosen to use it for good by making better moments for others.

I will continue to help breast cancer organizations make a positive impact in our community. It gives me another purpose and pushes me to keep going. I don't spend as much time thinking about the fact that I have cancer. Instead, I focus on being happy and alive! I feel truly blessed. I know God has chosen me to provide hope and strength to others that will be diagnosed with this disease. I want to feel that I made a mark before I leave, but I plan to keep going as long as I can!

I read this framed quote, by famous choreographer and dancer Martha Graham, every day to remind myself that I have a responsibility to the world to keep living my God-given purpose:

"There is a vitality, a life force, a quickening that is translated through you into action, and there is only one of you in all time, this expression is unique, and if you block it, it will never exist through any other medium; and be lost. The world will not have it [. . .]. You have to keep open and aware directly to the urges that motivate you. Keep the channel open. No artist is pleased. There is no satisfaction whatever at any time. There is only [. . .] a blessed unrest that keeps us marching and makes us more alive than the others."

And then I put on my stilettos, have a glass of wine, and thank God I am still here, thriving.

Susan Sullivan Danenberger

Susan Sullivan Danenberger is a 5th generation farmer, winemaker and the owner at Danenberger Family Vineyards. She is a 2x cancer fighter with stage 4 Metastatic Breast Cancer.

Susan has had to learn that living with metastatic breast cancer is a lot different from living after cancer, after my cancer returned. Her doctors have joked that her breast cancer journey is like a (bad) soap opera, because she shows up to my treatments wearing stilettos. In 2019, SIU School of Medicine sponsored her to walk in the AnaOno Cancerland NY Fashion Show, which shed a light on bra inclusive options for reconstruction and opened a whole new world of support from the MBC community. Her motivation to keep going is her winery, Danenberger Family Vineyards, in Central Illinois.

Connect with Susan at www.dfv-wines.com.

CHAPTER 14

A Journey of Love

Tamara L. Hunter

Don't cry because it's over. Smile because it happened.
~Dr. Suess

What is life and why, dear reader, am I asking you this at the beginning of my chapter? It is because I am going to make the case that if you are facing and embracing the impact of cancer, you have been given a priceless gift. The gift of understanding the importance of life.

My name is Tamara L. Hunter. I was diagnosed with *the breast cancer* towards the end of 2014. I am one of five people, all in one family line, that have heard *those three words*. Two gained their wings, my hero grandfather, and my mother. My only brother, my daughter, and I are all survivor-warriors. How can I feel good about sharing how *those three words* can be a gift? It is because I believe that too many are living their lives unaware of what is profoundly important. When you face death, you see life. My hope is that as you read this book, you take the pearls of wisdom shared by each author and reflect upon them. I want you to realize how every moment you are alive is a priceless gift and to live those moments full of love!

The Moments We Remember

Memory is the diary that we all carry about with us.
~Oscar Wilde

I remember the moments I heard *those three words* regarding each of my family members and myself. Could I share with you what the date was off the top of my head? No. Could I even tell you how old I was some of the times? No, I cannot. Yet can I tell you exactly what I saw, how I felt, what I did immediately after receiving the news? Yes, I can. It was like time stood still and imprinted these moments and memories upon my heart and mind.

When I received the call for myself, it was a beautiful day in October. At the time, I lived in Southern California. I had the windows open and was enjoying a cool breeze in the late afternoon. I remember standing there talking to the doctor. I did not cry because I already knew that I was facing a duck. You know, if it acts like a duck and quacks like a duck, it is most likely a duck. I knew I had a duck. Even to this day, I rarely use that six-letter *c* word. I say, yes, I was diagnosed with a duck. I refuse to allow *cancer* to have any power in my life. In fact, many know I will say, *Let's kick cancer to the curb*. When doing so, I motion at the same time using my hand as a foot kicking the *duck cancer* away to infinity and beyond. I refuse to give *it* any power in my life! My hope, dear reader, is that I will encourage you to do the same. *It* doesn't deserve your power. If you currently are facing a *duck*, kick it to the curb, too! Trust me, it may sound simple, yet you'll feel so much better. I bet you may even have a grin or smile once you do. And every time you feel you need to take back your power, kick it to the curb!!! It works.

Am I telling you I never cried? No, I am not. It is true I did not cry when I heard those words for myself. Truthfully, I knew I was going to be ok; it was only a duck! I did cry when I heard those words for my nineteen-year-old daughter. I also cried when both my grandfather and my mother gained their wings. Do tears negate my belief that having these experiences can be a gift? No, they do not. They confirm it.

For Everything There Is a Season

> *To everything (turn, turn, turn), There is a season (turn, turn, turn), And a time to every purpose, under heaven. A time to be born, a time to die… A time for love, a time for hate, A time for peace, I swear it's not too late.* ~A song sung by The Byrds, Written by Peter Seeger.

Peter Seeger wrote those words and The Byrds sung them in the 1960s when our world was in turmoil. On December 12, 1965, the Byrds performed *Turn! Turn! Turn!* on the CBS-TV program The Ed Sullivan Show. This was a time of unrest. The Vietnam War, Civil Rights, many assassinations, and so much more was happening. People were looking for relief from the pain. What is interesting is that these words were sung very close to exactly as they were written over 2000 years before.

The lyrics of Peter Seeger's song *To Everything There Is a Season* were taken word for word from the Bible (Ecclesiastes 3:1-8). The only words Seeger added were *Turn! Turn! Turn!* and *I swear it's not too late.*

Why is this so important for me to share with you? It's because these are timeless truths. And the moral of the story to both is that there are seasons in our lives. We will face a time to be born, and we will face a time to die. It is what we do during our *time to every purpose under heaven* that is key.

Your Life Review

I believe love is why we're here on the planet and that ultimately; it's our purpose for life. They say people who've had near-death experiences often report back that at the end of our lives we have a life review and we're asked one question, and that question is how much did you love?
~Marci Shimoff

Have you ever watched the movie *Defending Your Life* with Meryl Streep and Albert Brooks? As the story starts, the main character, Daniel Miller, isn't having a good week. For starters, he died after getting hit by a bus. Then he discovers he must defend his actions on Earth to ascend to a higher existence. One event after another continues to happen to Daniel throughout this romantic/comedy. In the end, well, you'll have to watch, I never give the ending of a movie away.

I love this movie. Yes, I love movies in general. Yet, the storyline shared gives you a lot to think about. Do I believe, as was shared by

Marci Shimoff, that at the end of our lives it is how much we loved that truly matters? I do. Did I before my experience with a duck pre-2014? Maybe not in the same way.

Doctors diagnosed me with HER2+, ER and PR negative breast cancer. I will never know for sure what stage I was at. They thought I was in stage 3. I was told my pathology report showed it was aggressive. I did six rounds of chemotherapy cocktail and a full year of one of my two immunotherapies. I had a double mastectomy, many reconstruction surgeries, and a full hysterectomy. I lost my hair, my toenails and fingernails, and my voice due to chemo sore on my vocal cords. I had huge open sores on my face. I bled from areas you do not want to bleed due to side effects. In fact, my doctor told me I won the award of all his patients for the most side effects he had ever documented. Due to major complications, I was put into ICU after one of my surgeries. I experienced so much pain that it was hard to make it through one second---one minute was way too much time to even think about. During my active chemotherapy, I was put into *solitary confinement* or isolation in my own home because there are four generations and too many people living in the home. This was pre-COVID. They did not want me to be around others while going through active treatment. So, why do I say all of this was a gift? Because it was!

My life changed during my treatment. I met a buddy during a horrible allergic reaction on my first day. I had fallen asleep. Through a fog I heard a voice that attempted to wake me up. That voice was off in the distance. It was saying, "Are you alright? Are you alright?" I tried to react to the voice and realized I could not open my eyes, my face was on fire, and my throat was closing. I could not speak. I was not alright. I remember putting my hands to my throat. From there all types of activity took place. My life was saved that day, it was the day that changed me. The voice was the daughter of whom became my original buddy.

I am not sharing this to scare you. I am sharing this because I made it. I knew I would. It was only a duck! The power of knowing and never doubting is critical to understand. Was it easy? No, it wasn't. Throughout the full time I knew what I was experiencing was only a small portion of my life. I knew without a doubt I could and would endure it. And I did. SO, CAN YOU!

My original buddy and I would travel our healing journey together for two years. That experience was to become the blueprint of my mission and purpose going forward---to let people know there is power in *healing through connections* and we can raise the frequency of the world through love.

Humor, Hope, Heart, Hugs, and a Whole Lot of Love!

We are the ones to change the world with our hearts.
~Tamara L. Hunter

What is important to you? If you are experiencing your own duck right now, how are you doing? I want you to take a moment and really think about it. Are you like I was, you know you've got this? Or are you experiencing fear, doubt, isolation, depression? Be honest. This will only work if you are.

Get out your journal or a piece of paper. OK. Now, I want you to write down or type who and what is important to you. Write as much as you can think about. If you have pages of answers, great. If you have only a few sentences, great. This is yours about you, today. Next, how are you doing? Why? How can it change? What do you want your life to look like post-duck?

In my Celebration Journal, I share some of my own experiences. I will share about one of my daily practices, and I encourage you to adopt it, too. I have been writing down each day what I am grateful for most of my life. I typically will record five people, places, or things. There were some days during my treatment that it was a stretch to record much, yet I always found something. This practice helped me when I had those moments. I would realize how lucky I was and how much of a gift my life is. Start writing down every day what you are grateful for and see how your life changes. It works!

If you are feeling alone, look up a support group community on the internet. They welcome all those facing cancer, all types, all stages, and other life-changing events, both the patient and those who love and support them. Do not face it alone!

Make Your Bed!

Making your bed to perfection each morning is a reminder that if you do the little things right, it makes the big things possible. ~Admiral William H. McRaven

---

Are you thinking to yourself, "I am recovering from illness and I am on bed rest," or "I will just be going right back into my bed, so why are you telling me to do this?" Because it works! I was not allowed out of my room within my own home for nearly six months during my active treatment. I did not spend time face to face with family, friends, or anyone else during that time. It was a very bad cold and flu year, and I was a high-risk patient. They would leave things outside my door and knock. I would go and get it after they moved away. They did not come into my room. No one else saw my bed. It was only me. Yet, I did make my bed every day! Then I would get back into it. The process of making my bed was the important thing in this practice.

In 2017, I started a nonprofit organization and by the time COVID started in spring of 2020 we had *buddies* throughout the world. I would go live daily during my morning walk. I would say at the beginning of each live, "Bed check, make your bed, change the world." Now, not everyone is looking to change *the world*. Yet, if I say it this way, "Make your bed, change your world." How does that feel? Yes, take your power back. And in doing that, you will start to see how much taking care of yourself through self-love helps. Remember, your life is a gift!

How Are You Sharing Love?

Where there is love there is life. ~Mahatma Gandhi

By realizing that love is the key to life, you find it freeing. Many of us complicate our lives in huge ways. I am so guilty of this fact. It is something on which I am still working. Yet, true unconditional love for ourselves and others can be simple.

I know that we all have a service hero inside! Sharing simple acts of kindness and service are ways to share love. Do something as simple as checking in on someone else that you might meet in treatment. Huge, that is love. Bring extra items in your treatment bags for others; that is huge and sharing love. Smile at someone that looks afraid and alone, again huge and an act of unconditional love. Tell yourself how much you love yourself and that you are worthy to get through this, huge and full of unconditional priceless love. Loving acts of service are priceless gifts of life worth sharing.

Do you need to forgive yourself for anything or to forgive someone else? Forgiveness can help us in so many ways. You may say something like "I will never forgive this person or that person. You have no idea what they did to me." No, I do not. Yet, I am not saying you must allow them into your lives if they hurt you in any way. Many of us have been through such horrible things. Yes, that is a common bond many of us have. The *Horrible Things Club*. Yet, you do not need to be a lifetime member. That is one membership you may want to do the work and let it go. Forgiveness does not mean forgetting! Practicing forgiveness is all about helping you to move on with love inside instead of the pain, fear, anger, or worse. I implore you to do the work. If you need help, reach out to someone you trust that understands the concept of forgiveness and letting go of what may be making you sick. Yes, it can make you sick! And if you are in the middle of recovering from a diagnosis, you want to allow yourself to be full of healing light and energy so you can heal!

I know about this because I did exactly this, too. It took me years to understand how important it was. I felt that in completely letting go *with love* someone that had nearly killed me, I would be somehow empowering the issue to do more harm. I was thinking backwards. Finally, when I let go with unconditional love and forgiveness, it changed my entire being. It freed me. The love inside of me and the memories that I chose to allow in are beautiful. Do I share much of this time in my life with much detail? No, I do not. Why? Because I know how important it is for my own health and how powerful words are in our lives. I am sharing with myself unconditional self-love. Do yourself a favor, try it out. In doing so, I believe you will find your way to peace.

Surprise, Surprise, Surprise No One Is Perfect! Not Even You

I don't know a perfect person. I only know flawed people who are still worth loving. ~John Green

Each day we wake up is an opportunity to give ourselves a gift. Eleanor Roosevelt was a woman that had influence during some tough times in human history. She shared a famous yet simple quote, *Tomorrow is a mystery. Today is a gift. That's why we call it 'The Present.*

How true! Today is a gift! And, if you are reading this that means you are alive. You may be experiencing one of the toughest times in your personal life or you may know someone that is, yet you are alive! By embracing the impact of living, your perfectly imperfect life is a priceless present, your own priceless gift. The time for change is now. Let go of the pain. Allow the love in. Spend every day of your life full of *every purpose under heaven.*

I told you at the beginning of this chapter that I was going to make the case that if you are facing and embracing the impact of cancer you have been given the gift of understanding the importance of life. My hope is that I have made the case. That you are now a believer, too.

I know beyond a shadow of a doubt that life is worth living no matter how painful, frightening, or unknown it may be for you today, you are alive. Being alive is an opportunity. It is up to you how you want to show up. My hope is that you show up, forgive, and love yourself and then find ways to do the same for others. In doing so, you may see that your frown may turn upside down, and you can smile that frown away.

As for me, I show up every day the same. I choose to live my life as a journey of love! My hope is you will, too!

Tamara L. Hunter

Tamara L. Hunter is a cancer survivor on a mission to change the world. She is the President and Co-founder of a nonprofit cancer support community. The *First Global Next Impactor*, CEO of Impactor Press and creator of My Big Dream Life Workbook and Journal Series. Producer and Host of multiple TV Shows airing on the e360tv network including her newest, *Let's Talk Fab...ulous with Tamara*. Three-time best-selling author. Keynote speaker, Emcee and Red-Carpet Interviewer.

Connect with Tamara at www.TamaraLHunter.com.

READER BONUS!

Dear Reader,

As a thank you for your support, Action Takers Publishing would like to offer you a special reader bonus: a free download of our course, "How to Write, Publish, Market & Monetize Your Book the Fast, Fun & Easy Way." This comprehensive course is designed to provide you with the tools and knowledge you need to bring your book to life and turn it into a successful venture.

The course typically **retails for $499**, but as a valued reader, you can access it for free. To claim your free download, simply follow this link ActionTakersPublishing.com/workshops - use the discount code "coursefree" to get a 100% discount and start writing your book today.

If we are still giving away this course by the time you're reading this book, head straight over to your computer and start the course now. It's absolutely free.

READER BONUS!

ActionTakersPublishing.com/workshops
discount code "coursefree"

Made in the USA
Middletown, DE
04 November 2023

41963036R00097